Listening to Students

Reflections on Secondary Classroom Management

Sue A. Thorson

University of Maine at Farmington

D1247328

Boston   New York   San Francisco
Mexico City   Montreal   Toronto   London   Madrid   Munich   Paris
Hong Kong   Singapore   Tokyo   Cape Town   Sydney

Series Editor: *Arnis E. Burvikovs*
Series Editorial Assistant: *Matthew Forster*
Executive Marketing Manager: *Tara Whorf*
Editorial-Production Administrator: *Beth Houston*
Editorial-Production Service: *Walsh & Associates, Inc.*
Composition Buyer: *Linda Cox*
Manufacturing Buyer: *Joanne Sweeney*
Cover Administrator: *Kristina Mose-Libon*

Library of Congress Cataloging-in-Publication Data

Thorson, Sue A.
   Listening to students : reflections on secondary classroom management / Sue A. Thorson.
     p. cm.
   Includes bibliographical references.
   ISBN 0-321-06397-X
    1. Classroom management. 2. Teacher-student relationships. 3. Middle school
teaching. 4. High school teaching. I. Title.

  LB3013.T58 2003
  373.1102′4—dc21

                         2001056625

Printed in the United States of America

10 9 8 7 6 5 4 3 2 1   06 05 04 03 02

Contents

Introduction

Within days of beginning to teach in a junior high school resource room, my authority was challenged when Art attempted to leave the classroom without permission. Fresh from an institutional practicum, I responded with a standard restraint. This action, which embarrasses me to this day, won Art's complete respect and the awe of my other students. Within two years, he had grown eighteen inches and gained more than one hundred pounds. The continued value of having the story of small, seventh-grade Art's attempted exodus recounted by big, high school Art was inestimable. By the time he graduated, my reputation was set for the next fifteen years.

According to the experts, my reaction should have established a conflict that would interfere with student learning until it was resolved. The contradictions between student reaction and academic theory have plagued me throughout my teaching career. I searched through conflicting theories of discipline, management, and control, trying different techniques and getting unexpected reactions from the students. The only consistency I saw was the inconsistency of responses from student to student and situation to situation. In a paraphrase of Freud (and with the same naiveté) I wondered, "What *do* students want?"

My experiences in the classroom gave some hints. Although a strong authoritarian approach did not work well for me, some students seemed to need clear boundaries and consequences before they could develop their own controls. Other students resisted rules, but responded quickly to positive reinforcement techniques. Our most comfortable and effective environments were centered in an atmosphere of mutual respect and curiosity as we learned together. It seemed, however, that as soon as we created that ideal learning environment, something happened to disrupt a student's life and we ended back at square one, with my instructional assistant and me trying to create order out of the ensuing chaos.

In addition to maintaining the kind of atmosphere we thought most useful for learning, my colleagues and I were concerned about the students' well-being. We wondered about the side effects of "effective" procedures. Every action we take results in multiple consequences for the student, the teacher, and the class. Efficacy *is* important, but what are we trying to achieve? What should we control? When? How? These questions, always important, become increasingly vital with the changing ethos of human interaction, the availability of efficient weaponry, and the current events in schools and on the streets. We need to understand what effects our casual and thoughtful reactions have on our students.

Since the experts couldn't agree, and we teachers couldn't figure them out, I decided to ask some students what they thought about discipline in schools. For my doctoral research, I talked to students about their perceptions of effective behavior management in high schools. I chose a Saturday detention to meet with a range of students, from habitual offenders to those who were caught in an atypical situation. This text includes the comments of fourteen students, who are introduced later in the text.[1]

The Book

The resulting conversations expanded my understanding of various classroom management techniques. I have added some research and referred to theories. I also included some of my experiences as a teacher. The result, I hope, presents a rounded picture of some adult-adolescent interactions in secondary schools. Although I include ideas about and references to a variety of disciplinary practices, this book is not intended to prescribe, but rather to provoke. It is my hope that educators will develop habits of thought and communication that will help them better prepare adolescents for life in a complex world.

As I wrote, I found it difficult to lay out the complexities of a classroom experience in a linear fashion. Time, teacher-student interactions, and life interweave to create unexpected situations. In order to capture these flying moments and infinite possibilities, I ordered the text in two layers.

Discipline and management seem to flow back and forth on a continuum of control, from teacher-centered to student-centered. These levels of control, when examined in isolation, generally flow on a timeline, from strong teacher control at the beginning of the year to increased student control by the end. This timeline also appears to be reflected in teacher practice; beginning teachers are often most concerned about and exert the most classroom control, while more experienced teachers are more relaxed. The students, the researchers, and I have had more experience with teacher-centered schools, so that is where most conversations are centered. As we approach a completely student-centered class, the hard data disappears, methods rely on serendipity, and conversations become wish lists. Perhaps the teachers in the twenty-first century will bring a change of focus and a new set of questions.

The text is divided into five parts: *Preparations*, about preplanning; *Beginnings*, about starting the school year and establishing a working relationship; *Progress*, about what might happen during the year; *Endings*, to consider the ideal classroom; and *Reflections*, to look back on the previous year before preparing for the next. In

---

[1]Parts of our discussion can also be seen in the November 1996 issue of *Focus on Exceptional Children*.

actuality, all of the events and conditions discussed can occur on the same day, in September, January, or June, together or separately. Control and structure are fluid, depending upon many factors, which is why good teachers are always preparing, reflecting, and adjusting.

The most critical factors in management planning are the relationships among teachers, students, parents, peers, and community members; the construction of rules, standards, and group values; the design of prescribed, motivating, practical curricula; and final results that influence the learning environment and the students we send into the world. Therefore, each section is divided into four sections, which address these issues, more or less in the order listed above. Again, none of this occurs neatly or chronologically. The teacher has to recognize where each student is, where the group is, and where the community is while everyone and everything seems to be changing.

I hope that the reader will interact with the book to create a moving image shaped by the participants, colored by current events, and paced by conflicting developmental, school, and social schedules. To this end, I have inserted many questions throughout the text. At the end of each section, I have described some activities suitable for preservice education students and, with some adaptation, for secondary content area classes.

The following text, then, is an attempt to synthesize research, practice, and student thought into a single conversation that will consider the following questions:

How do students perceive disciplinary procedures?

Which philosophy is most effective?

What kind of discipline policies are needed in schools?

How does discipline look in the classroom?

What suggestions about effective discipline do students have?

What's a teacher to do?

What *do* students want?

Acknowledgments

It is, of course, impossible to personally thank all of the people who helped with this book, because it is the result of some thirty years of teaching, which, in turn, is the product of a life.

My family, especially my parents, have been patient with me since birth. They taught me how to question, to think, and to question again, and insisted that I always respect others.

Good neighbors, Sue and Mick, responded, discussed, encouraged, and refused to let me waste the summer days.

My teaching colleagues, throughout my teaching career, have taught me about teaching, about contents, about kids. They have, as always, my respect and admiration. Sandra Schaal, Lani Martin, and Loraine Spenciner were, and are, of special help in my growth and survival as a teacher and writer. Mary Poplin, Lourdes Arguelles, Sally Thomas, Ray Glass, and Ann Lynch raise questions I continue to wrestle with.

I would like to thank the following reviewers for their time and comments: Jane Diekman, California State University, Stanislaus; JoAnn Hatchman, California State University, Hayward; Barba Patton, University of Houston-Victoria; Debbie Keasler, Southwestern Oklahoma State University; Jack V. Powell, The University of Georgia; and Elizabeth D. Primer, Cleveland State University.

Students have taught me the most, about teaching and living. My high school students constantly challenged the status quo and helped/forced me to grow beyond my assumptions about teaching and learning. My college students continue to challenge and encourage me to grow beyond my expectations. Robyn Weissman and Elizabeth Montgomery are two of many who have influenced this book.

The students whose comments are included in the text are all out of high school now. I thank them again for sharing their ideas, their feelings, and their brilliance.

Part I

Preparations

There's No Freeze Frame in the Classroom

It is critical to be an effective disciplinarian today, when angry youngsters have access to a variety of inconspicuous destructive weapons. Teachers deal with minor misbehaviors daily and now know that they may have to react to potentially lethal emergencies at any moment. Violence and opposition to authority are a reaction to school social controls that are perceived as unfair. Violence is seen as a means to higher status and power, often through the illegal acquisition of high status items such as cars, clothing, jewelry, and so on. Thus, violence can be seen as a way to achieve justice, control, and even self-help.

We all worry about how to "handle" the kids: how to control them, how to make them learn what they need to know, how to maintain a good learning environment, and so forth. But it's too late to create a discipline plan when a student is misbehaving. You can't put the student on hold while you figure out what to do, not only with the student who is acting out, but also with all of the others in the room; not only to solve the immediate problem, but also to avert future problems; not only to stop the misbehavior, but also to continue the learning process. Classroom discipline is a complicated process, filled with questions and disagreements, and affected by many factors. So, it is wise to think things through before you begin the year and then again during quiet times throughout the academic cycle.

When working with others, whether to teach, learn, or control, relationships are the most important factor. Good discipline and good teaching both stem from mutual respect and understanding. It is also important to have an academic environment, where learning is valued and facilitated. The teacher must create, identify, and maintain a safe structure so that students can develop a variety of skills and concepts. The curriculum itself affects the type and number of class management issues. Finally, a responsible educator must consider the results of the schooling process. Effective education does affect the student, who then affects the world. The behaviors and ideas learned in school are taken into society, where they influence adult goals, enhance or limit successes, and are then regenerated as students become parents and raise their children in the ways they themselves were taught.

Discipline, or student control, is a serious concern for most preservice teachers, an important issue for in-service teachers, and a major component of many in school administrators' daily activities. In the United States, it is perceived to be one of the biggest problems in public schools, regularly cited in Gallup polls. Discipline was the number one public concern for several years, but was replaced by a related issue, fighting, in 1998 (Rose & Gallup, 1998). The 2000 poll continues to raise lack of discipline as the second greatest public concern, followed by overcrowding, fighting/violence/gangs, and substance abuse (Rose & Gallup, 2000). The recent escalation of school violence has caused an increase in interest and opinions about disciplinary issues. When prioritizing problems in the schools, teachers rate discipline third, after alcohol use and smoking (Langdon, 1999), both of which require a discipline procedure in most schools.

After twenty years of teaching, I am still ambivalent about the "how" and the "when," but, like many teachers and administrators, I am convinced of the necessity for some type of discipline in the classroom. I've tried almost everything: parents' suggestions, various theoretical approaches, punishing, counseling, rewarding, ignoring, manipulating, listening. Everything worked sometimes, failed sometimes, and sometimes had totally unexpected results.

Theories of Student Management

Many modern educators have moral and ethical reservations about the use of punishment as a means to control students. There is no conclusive proof that punishment effectively controls behavior. On the contrary, there is a growing body of evidence that indicates that negative controls may actually increase discipline problems in some instances. Punitive consequences may actually exacerbate the problems of already rebellious adolescents and punitive procedures certainly contribute to a negative school environment, which indirectly relates to behavior in schools.

Although I was a graduate of a high school in which paddling was a part of the disciplinary procedure, my teacher preparation and basic psychology classes taught me how wrong a punitive approach was. In my first months of teaching at a public high school, I was appalled by the cruel attitudes of some of my colleagues. I tried to manage my students with a firm optimism about their abilities, three years of experience in an upper middle class private school, and an arsenal of behaviorist tricks. Then I took my students on a field trip. At the end of the school year.

After I smiled through a long, hot day of trying to herd twenty junior high students labeled with learning disabilities through a large city museum, the school bus driver dropped us off at the wrong school, promising to come back as soon as he finished his other runs. Half of the class then took off for home, while I fought with thoughts of liability and disaster. I established the shade of a large oak tree as a boundary, firmly requested the remaining students to stay there, and turned to confer with my aide. Immediately thereafter, I experienced my first surge of blood lust. I have no memory of what preceded the moment I still picture so vividly. I am standing in the bright sun, violently shaking Billy, an angelic-looking seventh grader, by the shoulders.[1] The shock of coming face to face with the violent side of my personality saved him from further physical retribution, but the strong emotional need to punish a child occurred regularly throughout my career. This action was followed by excellent behavior from Billy for the last few weeks of school, so it also seemed to be effective. During the next five years he became a favorite, often responsible, student, and continued to drop in after he graduated.

The following year, Cory joined the class. He was a gifted young man who did not develop according to national norms or learn according to the prescribed curriculum and methodology. He had spent three years in special schools before joining us in ninth grade. In the previous eight years, he had evidently learned how to drive adults crazy instead of learning to read; acquired superb debating skills while arguing his innocence in a variety of suspicious situations; developed acute observation abilities, enabling him to verbally skewer staff members with deadly precision; and generally became skilled at a variety of games of evasion and illusion that he played within the system. Punishment did not affect his behavior except to increase his anger and frustration.

So, I found that punishment either works or it doesn't work. It either makes students angry and resentful, or it doesn't.

Some theorists consider individual students and their human needs. They often believe that motivation and ego development are central to student manage-

---

[1]Geneticists have identified a "berserker gene" in people with northern European ancestors. Given the behavior of the Vikings in the first millennium C.E., I'll bet a lot of school teachers share this gene.

ment. Attention to these factors may be useful in a clinical setting, but when teachers are working with 150 to 200 students, each at a different level of development, but all bound to the same district or state-imposed curriculum, things get a little complicated.

Other researchers suggest that facets of society, such as home life or cultural background, are at the root of many resistant behaviors. Although logical, these rationales are not consistently supported by research or reality. No matter how relevant, there is not much educators can do to change the world outside of schools, although we have to deal realistically with the problems students bring in.

The educational institution is also blamed for problems with student discipline. Either too lax or too controlling, with curricula that are irrelevant or "fluffy," and environments that are physically dangerous or luxurious, schools are obviously doing something wrong. Although educators' best hope for student improvement lies in changing themselves and their procedures, recommendations to schools are often contradictory, quixotic, or unrealistic. It is difficult to imagine how the bureaucracies of schooling can change quickly enough to keep up with the rapid, comprehensive, and unpredictable changes of the modern world.

Developmental theories of behavior make current schooling practices seems hopeless. Teenagers are considered to be rebellious, need physical activity, have eating and sleeping schedules that conflict with school schedules, value fun over work, and see most curricula as irrelevant. Klaczynski (1990) suggests that education is not always important to adolescents; schooling does not meet their developmental needs. Fine's (1991) research in inner city schools indicates that school may actually contribute to dependent behavior, depression, and conformity.

In a secondary school resource room, I quickly learned about shaping adolescent behavior to meet my teaching needs. A combination of theories and practices worked most of the time, but there were always a few chronic discipline problems.

Daniel always challenged school policies in my room. He cut class one or two days a week, but when he was present, we often had violent arguments, with him hurling insults and books at me, and me responding with a furious "TO THE OFFICE!" I instigated many detentions and several suspensions for him. A few days before he graduated, he wrote in my yearbook:

> For 3 long years you put up with me. Thanks for all your help. You helped so much all these years. I don't know how to thank you. You pushed and pushed me until I did. I hope I can make you proud of me. I'll try my best. When I give up, I'll pretend that your fingernail is in my rib, making me laugh and jump. Have a nice summer, I don't want you to do no work. Just relax, you work too much. I'm really grateful for your help. You stood by me when nobody else would. At one time I thought about suicide . . . you knew I could make it so I believe you. I will try. You have that crazy idea . . .

Did Daniel and I have the same experience?

Efrem was a quiet young man who left a note on my desk stating, "Thanks for kicking my butt when I needed it." I asked him what he meant, and he reminded me of a long walk we had taken the previous spring, when he planned to drop out. My memory of the forty-five minute stroll around and around the school was of a caring, reasoned conversation in which we discussed his concerns and looked for ways to enable him to stay in school and graduate on time, which in no way resembled my idea of "kicking butt."

Rafe was obviously developmentally delayed. He looked and acted as if he still belonged in elementary school. He could not read, write, or sit still. We read to him and listened to him read; we taught him how to use a word processor; and when he disappeared up the air shaft, we coaxed him down. He graduated with some basic skills. The other students hated Rafe, resenting the extra attention and apparent leniency from the teachers.

So, discipline is necessary, but what works? I needed to figure some things out.

Building Relationships

There is a lot of talk about relationships, or more exactly, the lack of relationships in modern schools. Feminine pedagogy suggests that relationships are central to the type and amount of learning that occurs for many students.[2] In the Poplin and Weeres (1992) study of schools, many students expressed concern about relationships among students, teachers, and administrators on the secondary campus.

Thinking back, it is true that much of our classroom learning was rooted in feeling. As I tried to control them, I learned about life and classroom management from students who drove me crazy and from students I respected. Eventually, the two groups merged into a group of individuals whom I often admired, but who still had the power to drive me crazy. Teaching in a small school and then in special education gave me the opportunity to develop strong relationships with many of my students.

It is easy to *talk* about building relationships in the schools; it is not so easy to accomplish. The ratio of time to students makes it difficult for teachers to build a significant relationship with each student. Distancing also provides the teacher with protection from the horrible, insoluble problems some students bring to school.

One relationship that teachers rarely examine is the relationship with self. Again and again I watch potentially good teachers fail before they begin because of their own insecurities. Others burn out because they spend all of their energy on student needs rather than reserving time to take care of themselves. Beginning teachers, who had known only success as students, are discouraged by the failures that are part of every good teacher's day. Friendly people are crushed by adolescent anger.

So, before you begin, stop and admire yourself. Identify your strengths. What do you have to offer your classes? Your colleagues? Your community? How will you care for yourself? Set up a schedule for eating and sleeping according to your needs

---

[2]Mary Belenky, Blythe Clinchy, Carol Gilligan, Nancy Goldberger, bel hooks, Ted Sizer, Jill Tarule, and Nel Noddings are some people who write about the role of relationships in the teaching-learning process.

(plan on sleeping a little more that first semester). No matter how much you hate it, physical exercise can alleviate, and even solve, a lot of problems. Find a physical activity you like, or can bear, and pursue it compulsively. A little personal time will also help you get through the rough spots. Understand that time for yourself, time with your friends, and attention to your health will benefit your students and make you a better teacher because you will be capable of working at your best rather than constantly coping with your worst.

Go ahead, make some entries for you in your academic calendar *in ink*, and get ready for a good year.

Planning the Year

Now, make yourself comfortable and let your imagination run free. Unfettered by constraints of custom and budget, what would your perfect classroom be like? In your mind, create the space. What do you see? What do you hear? Are there smells, feelings, and other sensations present? How are they created? Add students to your place. What are they like? What are they doing? What are you doing? Gather some materials and try to recreate your image on paper or in a model. Choose some components to bring in to your actual classroom.

Much of curriculum is already assigned to us, by the content area, state standards, and district goals. Take some time to examine your requirements. Then consider your reasons for teaching a particular subject. How will it enrich the student's life? What skills will it develop? Look at the requirements of another subject area. What did you learn in that class that you use today? Reexamine your curriculum and goals. What will people not interested in your content area take from your course?

I also found it useful to block out a theme for the year—an umbrella under which all of our activities could be loosely connected. For example, we may have looked at history as a chronicle of change, or math as a way to establish some control in our lives. Many middle schools try to have schoolwide themes, such as environment or travel, each year.

You will have a few students who love your subject and will want to make it a lifelong study. Most of your students will feel neutral about the content, but will politely accept your direction and may be led to enthusiasm. Then, there will be those who, for one reason or another, resist and even combat your instruction, who see no value in the skills and concepts you have to offer, but may, by interesting activities, be enticed to learn. What do you have to offer each group?

Now is a good time to block out a calendar for the year that identifies the topics, skills, concepts, and activities you want to include in your program.

And then what? You have little say about who enters your class, but you have the opportunity to affect all of your students before they leave. No, you alone will not change the world, but you and your colleagues can, and will. Each teacher nudges students in a particular direction. Which way do you want your students to go? Who will be leaving your room at the end of the course? How will they make a living? What will they vote for? What will they fight for? What will they ignore? What will they understand? Consider your goals, and list ways to achieve them through relationships, environment, and curriculum.

Unfortunately, the best plans rarely come to fruition. Sometimes, we need to rejoice in the small steps we take toward our goals, and understand that the teaching-learning process is complicated and that implementation of ideas in the midst of coping with reality is difficult. We also need to realize that our students, colleagues, and community members have not read our plans and may not be working toward the same goals. Finally, we need to continually adapt our plans as we receive new information, change our perceptions, and react to a rapidly changing world. This means that preparation is a continuous process both throughout the school year and throughout a teaching career.

Some Activities to Try

I use many of the following activities in my undergraduate education classes. I have also either used or seen them used successfully in K–12 classes. They are useful in helping students begin to focus on a topic, to formulate tentative ideas, and to establish a foundation from which to learn.

Folder: Give each student a plain manila file folder. On the inside, have them draw simple pictures or create symbols about the content. Some students are more comfortable using magazine pictures. I ask preservice teachers to draw five symbols each about who, how, why, where, what, and when they want to teach, but in geography, the students can include land forms, economics, local shelters, and so on. As they work, I speak with each individually and, on the folder tab, write the student's name and group assignments in dark ink. They share their folders with the group, then I collect them and have them laminated. When I return them to the class, we discuss ways to help students and teachers organize class papers.

Calendar: In small groups, create a calendar of September lessons that will meet content instructional needs and establish a desirable classroom environment. This can be a variation of the KWL[3] method in K–12 classes.

Matrix: In content area groups, create a planning matrix on a piece of chart paper. Across the top, list all of your concerns as teachers: what you must "deliver" and accomplish. The list would include assessment, skills, information, concepts, and so on. Down the side, list all of the activities you can do in class, such as lecture, reading, videos, field trips, and so on. Mark the intersections of concerns and activities. How can you use this information?

---

[3]KWL is a useful way to begin a semester or a unit. Learners are asked to brainstorm what they know or think they know about a topic, what they want to know, and how they will learn and share their learning. Of *course* some students are going to say they don't know nothin' and don't wanna learn nothin'. They usually got caught up in the unit, especially after I gave them an unpleasant alternative (Thorson, 1995). Students who honestly thought they knew nothing and had no questions could be prompted with references to current media, a quick scan of the relevant text, or an Internet search.

Math

	Problem solving	Listening skills	Computation	Numeration	Assessment
Lecture		×		×	
Worksheets	×		×	×	×
Build paper monster	×		×	×	×
Measure hall	×			×	×

After discussing some class goals, students in content area classes could design a similar matrix to enhance a KWL activities.

Part II

Beginnings

Your first contacts with your class set the tone for the rest of the year. Your students want to know who you are, what you will offer them, and what they must give you. I once knew a young White teacher from a wealthy home took a job in an inner city school. She started her year with the Bill of Rights. Amelia tried to teach African American and Latino/a students—most of whom had family members in jail, many of whom belonged to local gangs—that the law and police force protect the citizenry. She passionately defended her position, supported by her own experience, that of her friends and family, and the textbook. The students, however, had grown up in a different part of the county and had different observations. At the time, the news was also full of unrest caused by the judicial process applied to White police officers being tried for undue violence in the arrest of an African American. Amelia lost her students that week, and, in spite of trying many different teaching techniques, she never regained their confidence or their respect, and so was plagued with behavior problems for the rest of the year.

Because relationships are so important, it is critical that you become acquainted with your students as quickly as possible. Getting to know one or two hundred individuals is quite a challenge, but there are some ways to facilitate the process.

Skimming through confidential files can give you an idea of past events and habits, but do not necessarily prepare you for the changes that may have occurred recently. For example, although there is some statistical accuracy, violent behavior is not predictable across time (Phelps, 2000). Contrary to popular opinion, violent youth do not always become violent adults. Vacations and transfers often cause unpredictable positive and negative changes in youth.

Some teachers do extensive pretesting to establish a baseline understanding of their students' academic skills, interests, previous experiences, and other strengths. While they write introductory essays, complete skills assessments, and fill out personal questionnaires, you have an opportunity to conduct brief conferences to establish contact with each individual. The students also want to know about you, so be ready to answer the same questions about yourself that you have asked them. They will also have other questions; some things you will enjoy sharing, other questions can be answered with a "No comment" as you protect your personal life. The questions you ask and answer will also give the students an opportunity to learn about constructive professional relationships before they join the workforce.

As you and the students beginning to form a working relationship, you will also have to establish parameters for the class. Think back to your planning in Part I. How will the class be run? What are the rules and consequences? What can you put up with? When do students have to change? How do your ideas fit in with the discipline procedures of your school?

At the same time, and perhaps of primary importance, you are responsible for instruction. What did you decide you want students to learn from their experience with you? What does the district expect them to learn from you? How are you going to teach them? In what order will you present material? It's time to earn your pay check!

Many educators believe that an important function of schooling is to train children to become responsible adult citizens. To that end, students receive mandatory classes in health and social studies. Teachers in all content areas enforce the rules and behaviors they believe to be courteous and productive. Teaching students how to live in the adult world is certainly a part of our responsibility. Who will you be sending into society? What will they believe to be their roles and responsibilities?

If you do everything exactly right, you will have the classroom experience you dreamed of, or so they say.

The next chapters introduce some students who have had a variety of public school experiences, some ideas about rules and curricular decisions, and possible results of traditional schooling procedures.

1

The Students' Point of View

*. . . I'm being here [in Saturday School detention] for the next three weeks. So if
it would have had an effect, then nobody would be here the second time.*

—Chaquan

I thought I yelled at Daniel too often; he remembered a caring supportive teacher. I
thought I communicated with Efrem in a mature, thoughtful way; he interpreted
our encounter more harshly. My aide and I had tried to meet Rafe's very special
needs; other students saw injustice and favoritism. There is obviously a huge
discrepancy between how my students and I interpreted our shared experiences.
Kreuter (1983) suggests that students and teachers perceive discipline differently,
while phenomonologists (Barritt, Beekman, Bleeker, & Mulderij, 1985) believe that
we all experience interactions in individual ways.

So how do students understand disciplinary procedures? Would their points
of view help identify effective techniques to manage behavior? "When researchers
have gone to the people they're studying and asked how it is, their research becomes
both relevant and honest" (Barritt et al., 1985, p. 14). Maybe I should ask some kids.
I selected detention as a place to begin for several reasons.

Having students stay after school is an easy way to arrange a private conference, tutorial, or makeup test. Often the experience is uncomfortable for the student,
and what is convenient scheduling for the teacher may be disruptive to the student's
schedule. Thus, throughout the years, "staying after," or "detention," has developed
a negative connotation and become one of the preferred methods of discipline in
secondary schools. Afterschool or Saturday detention is used as a consequence for
a variety of unacceptable behaviors, from tardiness to truancy. These behaviors may
be exhibited occasionally by "good" students and are frequently seen in "problem"

students, so I expected to find representatives of most student types in a detention situation.

Although discipline is ultimately about control, this control is rooted in understanding. You must understand your students in order to control them. I spoke with some high school students who had been disciplined in a Saturday School detention in order to understand their view of school discipline. Half were assigned to special education but had some general education classes. Although the students looked at discipline from different perspectives, many of their ideas paralleled current theory. Their ideas will appear throughout the text, so I will introduce them now. You may see students like them in your classroom.

The School

City High School is a large complex of long, single-story collections of classrooms located in a southern California city in the process of a dizzying, fifty-year change from orange groves to bedroom suburb to urban community. Its citizens are primarily working class.

The students discussed three types of discipline: ABC, Saturday School, and suspension. They were also very aware of when their parents would be contacted. Some ignored afterschool detentions with their teacher and so were assigned Saturday School. A few students mentioned more serious consequences stemming from expulsion proceedings.

Academic Behavior Center, or ABC, the in-school suspension program, was universally dreaded. Students described it as being like a jail, which they were not allowed to leave except at certain times. They could not socialize or talk at all, could not sleep or play games. They had to face the wall and do schoolwork.

The official detention program at City High School was changed at the beginning of the year from an afterschool detention to a Saturday School detention. Misbehavior in class could result in an afterschool detention with the teacher, but an office referral led to spending the period in the office or ABC, a parent contact, and Saturday School, a weekend morning detention. Students were routinely assigned to detention for being late to class, misbehaving, and leaving school without permission.

The Saturday after being assigned detention, students reported to an art classroom, promptly at 9:00 A.M., with materials for schoolwork. They could be dismissed from the detention room to a special Title I reading program or other supplementary work if they had permission from the activity supervisor. Otherwise, they remained in the room until 12:00, with one restroom break. The group was supervised by a soft-spoken, firm art teacher, who took attendance promptly and enforced his rules strictly. Students were permitted to talk quietly, listen to music with headphones, do schoolwork, or sleep, but the teacher preferred that they do schoolwork. He often talked with students about behavior in general, helped them start an art project, or allowed them to help him with art room chores, but would kick a student out for any disruption. The students seemed to appreciate his friendly manner and behave well; however, they described Saturday School as a boring inconvenience.

One- to three-day suspensions required the student to stay away from school. The students assumed that administrators believed they were at home under a parent's supervision.

Expulsion to a continuation school was mentioned, but seemed somewhat mysterious. One student also talked about the intervention of the court system and being threatened with a special camp.

In the school, I saw overworked, dedicated professionals trying to provide a quality education in a constantly shifting environment. What did students see?

The Students

Alissa

Alissa[1] is an African American senior in the college prep program. Initially she was reluctant to describe herself, but then became more specific:

> Me? What do you mean, by personality wise, or? I don't want anybody to know how I . . .! I'm quiet, but when I get an idea, or something like ignorance, that upsets me, I want to do something about it, I will not stop talking. I can talk forever! But most of the time I'm quiet. I like to read. I like to write. I just like normal stuff. Ice cream, Mexican food . . . Regular, but I got a lot of ideas, so . . .

Alissa believed that communication and understanding among students were lacking and was pessimistic about the potential for change:

> . . . there's not a lot of school spirit . . . there's not that many activities and when there is, people don't really know the purpose of the activity. It's like either to get out of class or just the fact that there's a longer lunch. It's not really to learn anything about anybody else, it's just, "Oh well, this is my free time." You know, it's a really selfish attitude, that's widespread in all the groups here.

She was frequently late for first period because her friends, who carpooled, were late in picking her up ("Not like by a big old time span. I mean, maybe right when the bell would ring and I'd have to run to class . . ."). When new rules were instituted, her mother insisted that she stop riding with her friends and walk to school instead. Now, although track, chores, and homework keep her busy until as late as midnight, she has to get up between 5:00 and 5:30 A.M. to get to school on time.

---

[1]At my request, the students described themselves and chose their own names. No student mentioned race or ethnicity.

> That's my whole schedule. I have to adjust everything around . . . I have to finish this, in enough time the night before, and do my chores in enough time and all that stuff, in enough time so I can get to bed so I can wake up the next morning on time, so I can get to school on time. Which is something that knocks everything out of whack . . . I can handle it. I mean, if it's up to me, I'll do my best not to be tardy. I won't purposely be tardy and say, "Oh, I don't care." I'll try my best, but I just think that, if something should happen, to where I can't get to school on time, that, you know, it's not up to me. It's not my fault. And I don't think I should be punished for it.

Alissa understood that important instructions might be given at the beginning of the period, but she had trouble getting to class on time. There were no lockers in the school, and hurrying around campus with the heavy textbooks for six senior classes at the college prep level often triggered an asthma attack. She began to keep some texts in the library, but going to the front of the campus between classes sometimes made promptness difficult.

Alissa was in Saturday School for the first time. She believed it was a waste of time. She didn't see it as a true punishment, because many people talked or slept. She was also concerned that people leave the experience planning to avoid getting caught in the future, instead of deciding to stop doing whatever they had been referred for.

For herself, she disliked the experience enough for it to act as a deterrent.

> I wanted to go to the Job Fair, or if I just wanted to sleep later, that it makes me mad. I did feel uncomfortable; it was an interruption. I feel like, if I broke the rules, I'm making somebody else uncomfortable, I'm upsetting, somebody enough to say, "Hey, you know, this isn't what you're supposed to do, whether you like it or not, and you have to go to Saturday School." And, I don't know. I learned my, I'm not gonna leave any more.

She saw the whole disciplinary procedure as another learning experience to prepare her for adulthood:

> Because we can only take what's there for us; if we find a way around it and change it and make it work for us, not necessarily hurting anybody, but, making it work for us, that's part of becoming an adult.

Alissa is like most students. She only needs one detention to learn that the rules are being enforced. With parental guidance, she changes her schedule to a more inconvenient, but effective routine that gets her to school on time. She seems to be fitting into the school society well, but feels it is sometimes unnecessarily difficult. What is she learning about life? How is she learning that lesson?

Ana and Robert

Ana is a Latina junior in special education. She is married to Robert, and they have one son. She wants people to know:

> that I changed a lot. That I'm more mature. That I'm a better person than I was before. You know, I might act weird sometimes, but you know, everybody acts weird once in a while!

After our first conversation, Ana told me her husband, a recent graduate of CHS, was very interested in the project. He joined us for one session. Robert was a 21-year-old Latino who, after leaving his gang, became actively involved in the community, working with the police to reduce graffiti in the city. He was an unemployed mechanic. He wanted to get more training and formal education, but believed his weak reading skills made that impossible.

When asked to describe the school to a newcomer, Ana said she would advise people planning to enter CHS to "turn around and run." She explained:

> Well, the people that go [to CHS] and stuff, the new people, they start hanging around with gangs. You know, taggers and, you know. You're gonna go to school to learn and stuff. You're not gonna go and be gangsters and stuff. And once you get hooked up with them, it's like . . . you just want to do whatever you want to do. I mean, if you're a good person, you want to stay with the good people, you don't want to be with the bad people. And act bad, and be bad when you're not. Try and be somebody else. You know . . .

Robert added, "If you're not in a gang, really, you ain't nobody." He still respected gang members, although when he dropped out of gang activities, he was pursued by gang members and feared death.

Robert and Ana were sure that there were guns on campus. Robert told of a classmate, since graduated, who carried a .22 handgun with her for protection after she was sexually assaulted, on campus, at gunpoint. She did not file a formal complaint because "she was scared. I mean, he was a gang member, who wouldn't be scared?" Both wish they could afford to send Ana to a safer, private school.

In spite of their fears, they did not believe security should be increased. They laughed about shared memories of running from the police.

Ana was disciplined by the school because she was caught at a "ditching party." Smiling, she recounted how she hid during the first raid, caused by a neighbor's complaint about noise, but was caught by police during the second raid, allegedly to search for a prison escapee. She and some other students were returned to school where a group picture was taken and later published in the local newspaper.

Both believed that too much money was being spent on ineffective security procedures. Robert mused, "But look at the money they're putting in this wrought iron fence. I mean, I think the wrought iron fence was uncalled for . . . That's a prison, you know." They evaluated suspension, both in and out of school, as boring rather than punishing, an inconsequential reaction to students' attempts to have a little fun.

Both Ana and Robert are the type of students who evoke much head-shaking in the Faculty Room. They're "good kids" who were caught up in the "wrong crowd." They are trying to change, but do not seem to have good role models. Why is their view of the school so different than that of Alissa and the other students? Which is accurate? Why do you think so?

Angela

Angela is a first-generation African American. Her family is from Ghana. She is a college prep junior who referred Alissa to the study.

> I don't want anybody to think I'm conceited or anything, but I think I'm smart, and nice. (Mischievously) Some people don't think so, but I do. But then I can be sensitive sometimes . . . People think I take stuff too seriously sometimes. So it's like, when they tell me stuff and I get mad, they just want to leave me alone after that, and they don't want to talk to me no more, cuz they think that I might, I don't know, say something to them . . . So I don't know if it's good or bad. I want to be a doctor. I have a long, long way to go. . . . My mom wants me to be a nurse. She thinks that would be easier for me instead of being a doctor. But I said, "No, I want to be a doctor."

Angela thought the school was improving every year. She appreciated the new paint and the recently installed air conditioning. She pointed proudly to the new classrooms and restrooms. But Angela is bored with school. She wonders:

> . . . how you can keep students in school, cuz . . . I know everybody, even if you're smart, even if you know that you need to be in school, you still don't like school. The only part you like about school is socializing with your friends and stuff. That's about it. All the work you have to do and everything. Unless the class is fun or something like that; maybe a few wouldn't mind going to class. Because I notice that people do that. The classes that they like, they go to, but the ones they don't like, they ditch. (It should be) a little more interesting. Cuz some teachers just give you book work. They just give you the work; they say, "Here, this is what you've gotta do; do it." And . . . that's boring.

Angela had trouble getting started in the morning when she stayed up late doing homework the night before:

> I'm tardy. To first period. Well, I'm not tardy that much. It's like, maybe like a minute or so . . . I don't know, you just can't help tardies, cuz tardies, everybody's gonna be late . . . I just can't get ready on time . . . I have an hour and thirty minutes to get ready. But sometimes I just sit there, cuz I'm tired, and I don't really get ready until the last minute, and that's why I'm tardy sometimes.

Instead of staying home, however, Angela now has her father write her an excuse so that she does not have to miss class. She realizes that she had a responsibility to find out what she missed and to not disrupt the class with her late entry.

Although she planned to not repeat her offense, because she did not like to waste a Saturday morning, Angela sees that detention is not a deterrent for everybody. She thinks the other students just don't care. She wonders if a more severe punishment would help, but is pessimistic about the potency of outside influence.

Again we see a student who has learned her lesson, although perhaps not in the way the authorities had planned. Mature enough to take responsibility for the classes she missed, and clever enough to avoid future detentions, Angela does not have to change her behavior. How many students find ways around the rules? What are they learning about life? Do you see adults who have learned this lesson?

Antashia

Antashia is an African American college prep student. She is a junior who has a reputation for being a responsible student; she is both an aide in the office and for a gym teacher. She says the important thing to know about her is that, "I try to do the right thing, mind my own business."

Antashia was assigned to Saturday School because she left school for a part of the period that she was a teacher's aide. She was careful to take roll and see if the teacher needed her for anything before she left to walk around the campus, help out in the office, or run out for a snack. She always returned in time to help the teacher clean up. On this occasion, she was seen by a proctor while entering her boyfriend's car. The proctor sent her back to class and checked on her a few minutes later. Unfortunately, Antashia had already left campus again. She felt her actions were perfectly normal, illegal only because she was not yet a senior, with senior privileges.

Neither Saturday School nor ABC would stop Antashia from repeating her offense because she did not feel she did anything wrong. In fact, she was indignant about her referral.

> I mean . . . to me . . . I don't think I should have Saturday School compared to what some of the other students do here. Like, when we have riots[2] and stuff, the kids that were involved in the riots, still go here, they're still walking around campus, whatever. They're not in Saturday School today, or any other day . . . OK, I left to go get something to eat, OK, punish me. But when people fight and everything, half the time they don't even get suspended. It was a fight last week, two girls, they didn't even get suspended Thursday. They was at school Friday. And I'm in Saturday School today (April 30), from something that happened on the fourth of February?

---

[2]During the year we met, there were several campuswide disruptions, which the students and faculty referred to as riots. Student descriptions of the riots can be found on pp. 120–125.

She thought Saturday School was "boring, tiring, and a joke." she continues:

> I mean, Saturday School, to me, and probably to basically everybody else, was just like, "Oh, I'm not gonna go to class. I can just go and get that little detention over with in Saturday School." . . . It's no big deal. . . . It wouldn't stop me from doing the things that I do, even though I don't do anything . . . (*But if you felt like doing something? . . .*)[3] Yeah, it wouldn't stop me. I wouldn't be like, "Oh, I'm going to . . ." I'll go to Saturday School. It's like waking up at, what, nine in the morning, to twelve. You're not doing nothing anyway, but sit at home and watch TV or listen to the radio, and you can do that here, except watch STV. You know, it's the same thing.

She stayed out of trouble because of her own standards, not from fear of punishment. She reiterated:

> Because you're supposed to come here and get an education. If you're tardy and you're ditching, you're not getting it. You know . . .

Antashia is an independent young woman, but many of her goals fit well in the institutional ideal. She is focused on getting a good education and being a responsible citizen of the school community. Why is she getting detention? Will it work for her? What is she learning about citizenship?

Carla

Carla is a 14-year-old Latina transfer student. She is in tenth-grade special education. In our discussions, she referred to friends who smoke, drink, and do drugs on campus. She has a clear understanding of herself in school:

> Well, I'm not a good student. I'm not a, you know, no school girl. I'll get in trouble sometimes, get suspended, and do like other people do. I haven't never seen a student at the school that would never get in trouble or get suspended or anything like that. I don't think there is a person . . .

Carla complained at length about the boring, repetitive nature of her classes. Her special education reading class did not provide enough help. She observed that she was still doing fourth-grade math in special education, while at home she helped her mother with the budget and did her sixth-grade sister's work. She was told she had to take summer school classes to make up for some courses she had failed and others she had been kicked out of, but the courses she needed were not offered, so she was scheduled for another remedial class.

---

[3]My questions will be noted in parentheses and italics when they affect the direction of the conversation.

Carla preferred to avoid a fight, but her friends literally pushed her into one with a girl from another group:

> . . . She was teasing me, you know, "Yeah, I have a boyfriend," and everything. And that day she was walking and she was talking about me, and I was gonna push her, but then I went "No," and my friend pushed me into her. And then she turned around and she was gonna sock me and I just started fighting with her . . . She turned around and she swanged at me. And I went back, you know. I had to do something. And I fought with her.

Returning from that suspension, Carla was then assigned Saturday School for talking back to her teacher:

> Because I have a problem reading and everything . . . and I'm embarrassed to read in front of anybody, even my mom. And she, my teacher, knows that I don't know how to read that much. And she just had me read and you know, she never asked me to read; she asked me to read sometimes, but in front of her. For her to hear me. And at that time, I was in a bad mood and everything, because I had just gotten in a fight the day before that and I got suspended, and like that was the first day I got back and then I got Saturday School. . . . She didn't get mad at me, she told me, you know, she got me a referral and everything. She didn't give it to me in front of the class. When the bell rang she gave it to me and I had to go to the office. And I got mad, you know, because, it just wasn't my day that day.

Instead of excusing herself, she tried to explain the teacher's normally understanding behavior. Carla knows she might have handled the situation better, but she had already been in trouble and just couldn't figure out how to avoid being embarrassed, except by defying the teacher.

Carla believed that ABC was, in fact, very punishing.

> You, like, when you come out of there, you're all, you know, "Ooooooh, I came out!" and stuff, but it's real (punishment) . . . Cuz you don't, you don't go out to lunch, you don't go out to break, and when you go to the restroom, they take everybody to the restroom, not only you.

Nonetheless, assignments to ABC would not stop Carla from repeating behaviors she did not view as being wrong. Saturday School was also not effective in preventing problems when the student saw no other way out. Carla added that, although some people seemed to be affected by these consequences, many people just did not go to their assigned Saturday Schools or ABC times. She thought the inconsistent reinforcement of the rules and consequences reduced the efficacy of the discipline code.

Carla believed that suspension caused more problems than it solved. Besides missing class work:

When they suspend you, you get in more trouble, cuz you're out in the street. And then the cops could stop you and you could just say, "Oh, yeah, they suspended me." And, you know, when they do that, sometimes they don't believe you, and sometimes they do. And when they don't believe you, they call the school and they get your i.d. number, and they'll ask whoever, you know, like the attendance, and she'll say, "Yeah, she's suspended; he's suspended." And that's what happened to me once, . . . I got into trouble one day cuz there was a party and they arrested everybody in that party; cuz there was a d.p., a ditching party, and that day I got in trouble more than I get in trouble at school, because I got arrested and everything.

She added that suspension also has a purpose:

. . . Just keep those kids away from the school. Cuz they [adults] can't handle them, they can't do nothing about it, they just tell them to stay home. They don't know what to do. They don't, [they] just say, "Oh yeah, you're suspended for three, four days." And just call your parents to tell the parents, and that's it. That's all they do.

Carla's attitudes about school are pragmatic and fatalistic. Although she understands the educational purpose of schools, she does not feel she is being educated. She is just putting in her time, because she doesn't know what else to do right now. What has given Carla these ideas? Are they, in her experience, justified? What does detention teach her? What predictions do you make about her future? How does that affect how you work with her? Why?

Casper

Casper is a European American in tenth-grade special education classes. He is generally extremely talkative, but had trouble describing himself. He said, "[I like] basketball and football. . . . I can do o.k. (in school) if I'm not with the wrong crowd."

Casper was concerned with understanding the rules at his new school:

I don't know the rules and stuff, so I don't think I'll be getting in trouble, cuz I don't know, like how many times you can get in trouble and be out of school, cuz that's all I need is to be kicked out of school or something. Cuz I've been, I don't really want to get kicked out of school.

Although he did not mention being concerned about safety while he was on campus, Casper was being harassed on the way to school because someone said he was talking about the leader of a group. He confronted the other youth when they were alone, and the boy backed off, but when the group was together, he was teased and threatened. He was concerned because he thought he might have to involve some of his friends in a face-off, or even a fight, to resolve the issue. He was not interested in bringing the situation to the attention of adults. Avoiding the group contributed to, but was not the sole cause of, his habitual tardiness.

Casper, however, took responsibility for his lateness. "Sometimes in the morning, I'll stop off at the doughnut shop. Then if you don't watch the time, you miss first period." He thought it important to be prompt so that you didn't miss time in class and eventually lose the credits you need to graduate. He hoped the stricter tardy policy at CHS would help him get to school on time.

Casper used to get in trouble because of an ongoing problem between the class and the teacher in his former school:

> Sometimes, when the teacher would be on the phone, we knew she'd be on there for a while, so we'd start talking, "What are we doing tomorrow; what are we doing now," and talk around and making jokes and stuff . . . Then like we'd get loud and stuff. And she'd like, "I'm on the phone!" And some kid would come out with a smart remark and stuff. And she'd like, "Who said that?!" And she'd turn her back so she didn't know who it was, and we're, "We don't know." . . . It's like, if we're just sitting there, we can't, if we're sitting there and everything, and she's on the phone, we're not learning anyway, so we start talking in a group . . .

Another time, he was blamed for turning out the lights because he had been out of his seat, throwing something away.

> Oh, I got Saturday School for it. . . . And then I tried talking to her calmly, I calmed down, cuz first I started yelling. And I calmed down, I was like, "Can I talk to you?" And she was all mad, "Oh, I don't want to talk to you right now! I don't have time! You guys always do this!" And then I was like, "Oh" (shrugs). And then I'm not gonna snitch on my friends, especially there, cuz then you have problems with them, so I just . . .
>
> I explained that to the principal and it's like, can't really argue with the teacher, then she's just gonna put more on the list.

Casper believed he had, at times, been blamed unjustly and explained how the office personnel tried to trick him into admitting that he was involved:

> One time someone threw a stink bomb in the class and we didn't even know who did it, someone turned off the lights, they threw it in class, and everybody outside was searched. But see, the person who did it only had one . . . Actually, they tried blaming the other kids, and they were like, "We didn't do it and we don't know who." I knew who did it, but I was like, "I don't know who did it." They called me in the office and they called me outside and they're all, "Four other people told me that you did it." So I'd say that it was him. I was like, "It wasn't me." Then I went back to class, and I was like, "They're gonna tell you that four people told on you that you did it." So then he went back, another kid went outside, and did the same.
>
> Yeah . . . And then sometimes a security guard walked in, he wouldn't say nothing, and then we're like, "Don't say anything!" And we'd tell it and they'd be like, "Well, I didn't do it." So we didn't get busted. We all got Saturday School, but I didn't go.
>
> . . . They tried to keep us all in the class and we all walked outside. The whole class was outside . . . and the teacher's like, "Get in here!" And we're like, "Sorry, not until you clean up that mess." And it still smelled! So, "I'm calling security on all the ones that are out there. Getting you searched."

He also told of a time when he was blamed for playing with the typewriter, causing the bell to go off. He admitted he had accidentally done it once, but his friends had continued to play with it. The teacher blamed him, and when he tried to explain, accused him of lying to her. She had security take him to the office, but after he left the room the bell went off again. Casper believed teachers suspected him because of his bad reputation and the friends he hung out with.

> But when I'm by myself, I'm like, I can be a new person. . . . Like in this class now, when I started here, I didn't hardly get in trouble at all, I have no problems with the teacher, and he gives me my work. No kids there to distract and do this, "Let's flip off the lights," and do all this other stuff and stuff. But like now it's like, I won't do it any more. With the new environment it's a new start. And I don't want the reputation I've got down there, where all the teachers say, "Yeah, that's Casper. Look out for him. He's always getting in trouble."

He was determined to build a new reputation in the new school.

Casper maintained that suspension was like a vacation, although being home alone all day could be boring. Even the threat of continuation school had advantages, because it was only one-half day long. He was not affected by school controls until he was taken to court. There he was given a strict set of rules to follow. Missing any school would result in his being sent away to a Youth Authority Camp, which he did not want.

Casper is the kind of student who drove me crazy. Obviously intelligent, but with poor academic skills, the only thing he had learned in school was how to have fun, at the expense of everyone else's educational experience. He is actively involved in a school game, adults versus students, which he is determined to win. How do you teach a kid like this? Does he belong in school? What are the alternatives? What predictions can you make about his future at City High School? As an adult? Why do you think so?

Chaquan

Chaquan, an African American student, was repeating general education ninth grade because she often chose not to do the work, which she found to be too easy. With the exception of a few classes, school was boring for her. She was outspoken and impulsive, blurting out, "I don't like this school, because the principals don't care." But Chaquan was not merely reacting to unwelcome constraints, she had thought about rules and consequences and saw their necessity in some instances. She thought, however, that the discipline at City High School was out of control. There were too many rules; the system was too confusing:

> Because on the first one [offense], you're dazed. I mean, then they go so far, the first one you're supposed to tell them, or talk to them, [but] they're ready to give you a referral or detention, right away. I don't like this school.

Chaquan's mother brought her to school, and sometimes her little sister made them late. Because of this, she was dropped from her first period class and lost the credit. She said, "They shouldn't give us referrals and all that for first period, cuz everybody's gonna be late. That's not gonna change. I don't know why they're doing it. It won't change for me." Being disciplined for talking was also a problem for her:

> I think you should be able to talk in class if you're doing the work, if you're done doing it. But during a test you shouldn't be talking, but if it's like class work and you discuss it, you should be able to talk. I mean you know how to do it, and you guys are working, and every few problems you stop and talk, and then you do your work.

Chaquan believed she received this detention because the teacher deliberately got her in trouble. "I got a referral from a teacher; she told three lies on me." She explained:

> I went to the nurse. And when I went in she told me to get a pass, so, the tardy bell had rung on my way to class, and I went, she was like, "Go get a pass." And I went to the nurse and I told her to call the teacher because she didn't believe I was in the nurse's office. And the teacher said that the nurse said to me not to come back to the nurse's office and the nurse never said nothing like that. The teacher said I always want to go to the nurse, and that's not true, because I never asked before in her class. So I don't know, I don't even know why she did that. And she wrote me a referral because I was sitting outside, and I walked out, I was laying on the bench, I needed to lay down, because I didn't think I couldn't go back to the nurse . . . And she wrote me a referral! I was like, that's not, and she said I always ask her to go to the nurse. I only been to the nurse twice this year and it was in third and fifth period, it was never in her class. She must have me mixed up with somebody else.

Chaquan did what she thought was sensible—went to the nurse when she was feeling ill. When believing herself to be forbidden to go to the nurse, she left the class and lay down on a bench outside. Upon reflection, she decided to speak to the teacher on Monday, but she had already had to go to Saturday School.

It seems obvious that Chaquan is going to have trouble throughout her school career. She has considered the requirements of the institution and found them to be inappropriate for its goals. She is not a "troublemaker," but she is resistant to assimilation by the school culture. Does she have the right to make this decision? What is the school's responsibility? What do you think is going to happen to Chaquan? What factors influence your predictions?

Don

Don is an African American in eleventh-grade special education. When asked to describe himself, he replied,

> Well, most people that I talk to say that I have a very good sense of humor, a very good mind of my own, you know, smart, talented, all of those things . . . I'm sixteen,

> gonna be seventeen. . . . I'm a very good artist . . . [I want to be a] lawyer . . . Because
> . . . if someone in my family needed an attorney, I'll be their attorney.

Don enjoys school, but would like to see the campus cleaned up a little more. He
thinks students could participate in cleanup, painting, and other beautification
projects. He would like to be involved in painting some murals on the exterior walls.
He believes that the student's attitude is important:

> Well, first I would say, it's a fun place to be if you really come to learn. And then it
> can be a bad place if you're not here to learn. Cuz then all your fun is problems and
> fights and, you know, all this kind of stuff, trying to get in gangs; you know, stuff
> like that. But if you come to school, mind your own business, go where you gotta go,
> get to that class, you won't have no problems. You be like, block out everything else,
> get right to class, get to your studies. Bam! You ain't gotta worry about no problems.

Although a change in attitude has helped him improve his behavior, Don still
has problems because, he thinks, he was in the wrong place at the wrong time when
he was kicked out of class. Once it was "cuz my friend, he kept laughing, right. And
I just sniggered one time and she thought it was me, so I got kicked out." Another
time, he had his book bag on his desk:

> . . . and they thought that I had a radio. Cuz my friend had his, and he was listening
> to his, and I was like, had my book bag up. The teacher thought I was blocking for
> him, so he thought I had my radio, so we got kicked out of class and then the principal
> took his radio and sent both of us to ABC and he gave us a Saturday School after that.

Don believed that he was being given another chance to avoid suspension and "they
(could) think you need time off from other students. You need to be in a quiet place,
somewhere by yourself."
He had a relaxed reaction to Saturday School:

> It's, Saturday School's like some come do work, but most people fall asleep, cuz you
> know, like, sitting in there so long, you be like, three hours, early in the morning, you
> fall asleep. But me, I just sit there, you know, just look at people; there ain't nothing
> to do in here, so . . . I guess that's mainly what Saturday School is all about. Sitting
> there and ain't doing nothing. Well, most people do stuff, but it's just, they just read,
> or some people play their Walkman, but I just sit there.

In spite of this opinion, Saturday School really stopped him because he did not like
getting up so early on Saturday morning. His feelings were ambivalent, however,
because he preferred Saturday School to in-school suspension. He preferred either
to home suspension and believed his experiences were helpful.

> Just to get away from the students, and you know, keep you by yourself in a quiet
> place . . . it helped me a lot. Cuz I'd be like, "Man, I gotta do better so I won't go back

in here no more. I miss all my friends." . . . Kinda like a little jail. Not a bad one. It's just a place to keep you until you think you have learned your lesson, not to get in trouble, not to be bad, talk back to the teachers or anything.

Don is an optimist, easy-going, relaxed, and helpful. I sensed that he was careful to tell me what he thought I wanted to hear, but his behavior did not reflect his discussions. In class, he continued to be tardy, aggressive, and late with assigned work. Why is there such a discrepancy between Don's statements and his behavior? Is it planned or does he misperceive his behavior? Why do you think so? How might his communication habits affect the student-teacher relationship?

Johnny

Johnny is a 16-year-old Latino in eleventh-grade special education. He describes himself as

> just a regular kid. I just don't behave, sometimes I behave bad, sometimes I don't. [This summer I work as] a janitor at San Jose Elementary School. [In my free time, I like to] go places with my friends, you know.

Johnny likes school work, especially if he gets enough help. He also enjoys the opportunity to socialize with his friends.

Johnny was kicked out of class for someone else's misbehavior, at a time he himself was trying to behave:

> Well, he kicked me out of his room, but I didn't do nothing wrong. The rest of the kids were messing around and throwing stuff at the . . . and I wasn't doing nothing. Only once, I made a noise and then, "Stop it, Johnny, stop it." And then, well, I said, "I'm sorry." And then I stopped it. And then, another kid make a noise and he thought it was me, so he kicked me out. So I said, "perro" [dog] to him because it's not right, because he didn't kick them other kids out, because they were making noise.

His friends tried to support him, but:

> So my friend, he told them who it was, it was him, and . . . they suspended *me*, but it wasn't me . . . they just suspended, they didn't listen, they don't trust kids, man. I just hate him; I hate that principal. I don't like him.

Another time, the teacher misunderstood him:

> . . . she said I cussed her out, but I didn't cuss her out. I was cussing this kid out. And she thinks I cussed her out, but I didn't. I didn't say her name. I just said this kid's name. So I got in trouble, I got suspended for two days.

Sometimes he did not understand the rules:

> The teacher for ABC, I wasn't doing nothing, she didn't, well, it was the first day, I think. Yeah it was the first day. She didn't give me no warning. She just give me, she says, "You're not doing no work. So, another day of ABC." So I had to stay in on Friday. So, o.k. Well, she's just supposed to give us a warning, so she didn't give me no warning . . .

When he and his friends did not understand the directions in physical education, the boys were punished, but not the girls.

> Another day (I got ABC) for not following rules in PE. Well, I did follow. He told us, "Go around." Well, around where? And so, he let all the girls off the hook and all the guys went to ABC. And like, that's it. That's how I got in trouble.

In spite of participating in the P.E. activities, Johnny was often in trouble because he did not dress properly.[4] "Gray or red. Or red and gray. That's o.k. Why I can't wear gray and gray, I don't know. He just gets mad. So I don't know what it's about."

Although he tried to behave, apologizing when he was in error, Johnny believed he was often disciplined because teachers misunderstood his behavior.

Johnny often had detention for being tardy, because he had to stay up late to let his father into the house, and then he overslept. Ditching was also a cause for conflict with authority figures:

> Sometimes it's good. Sometimes you get bored in school, so you have to go somewhere. I don't know, you just have some fun. Not putting pressure, if you want to ditch, you ditch. There's nothing . . . you miss only one day or two days or three days. That's it.

He has also received detention because he kicked a student who said something about his mother.

After five days of in-school detention, "You get crazy, you can't handle it. It's too much," Johnny said. A detention experience was punishing to him, and made him want to behave better, but he wasn't always able to follow through. Sometimes he thought twice about a fight, he forgot about the consequences until it was too late.

Johnny's accent and attitudes suggest that he and his family are maintaining their Mexican culture as well as living and working in the United States. Many of his punishments are a result of cultural misunderstandings and resistance to assimi-

---

[4]Certain types, colors, and designs of clothing could not be worn. Wearing the wrong clothing could result in being sent home, receiving in-school suspension, or confiscation. Some items, such as belt buckles with initials on them, were thrown away, because they were gang related. Specific outfits were required for physical education. The wrong gym clothes could result in a reduced grade.

lation by the school culture. Is acculturation a requirement for receiving a free and appropriate education in our schools? Which values and customs is it acceptable to maintain, and which must be ceded by members of nondominant cultures? Why? What is the school's responsibility? Why do you think so?

Nivek

Nivek, a Latino, dropped out of school in the tenth grade, before we completed our discussions. He dressed in a modified punk style, but did not want to be identified with any type of group. He was in a special education class, where "I'm not learning nothing!" He no longer studied because the teachers didn't teach too much, and he got confused trying to figure things out.

Students who are often disruptive may be labeled as "gangsters" in the school. "They don't respect nobody. They just do it." Nivek is quick to state that he doesn't like students with a bad reputation, and he doesn't hang out with them. "They just mess around the school and everything like that. They don't like to do anything on school, they just want to kick back, do nothing. It's a shame about them." Nivek also felt that part of the problem was caused by students.

> [Some] students . . . don't respect nobody. Just because they're in high school, they think they're all cool and everything. . . . I just . . . go. Just get it over with and do what you have to do. But the hate around the school, the racial stuff, the teachers, the mess around the school. . . . I see it everywhere. People stares at you, give you this bad faces, bad, some sign, some nasty sign. And they say bad things. . . . When I walk around, they just give you these bad old moods and everything like that. I don't like that.

Nivek got detention because he was trying to locate an open restroom, but was referred to the office for ditching:

> I got it because I was just walking around the school and everything like that. Around third period cuz I went to the restroom. And the proctors, they didn't believe me, that I had a pass, or something like that. I went back to class. But they sent me, like you have to go to ABC class. ABC you can take any time, so they sent me right there. So I got mad about it, so when I went to ABC class I was all mad. And they told me, "You better calm down." I said, "No. It's not fair just bringing me over here, just cuz I went to the restroom." . . . so they gave me Saturday detention because I wasn't supposed to be mad. This is a weird school, man. (*Well, when you got mad, were you swearing or yelling or stuff?*) Yeah, I swore some few couple of words, that's it. But I was frustrated after . . . cuz it's not right to do something like that . . . it wasn't that bad, cuz the teacher asked me for a pass; I said, "No, I don't have one. The teacher told me to go over there to use that bathroom."

Although he was angry about receiving it, in-school suspension "wasn't that big a deal. It's like wasting one day . . . It's not even fun. Just gotta stay there and do some work, that's it. It's so boring."

Nivek tried to fit in, couldn't, so he left. Is that acceptable? What are the alternatives? Why do you think that? How have other high school outcasts reacted to similar feelings of exclusion?

Rebecca

Rebecca is a 16-year-old Latina in eleventh-grade general education classes.

> I want to go to college or university . . . I want to study zoology . . . I was also thinking maybe I should go to the First Army Reserve. But, I still have to learn more about it. Find out what it's about . . . And after that, I don't know . . . [My personality is] I'm friendly, I'm nice I guess. Sometimes I could stand up for what I believe in, I like to help others, kind of like, community, church, homeless people, I like doing that. And volunteering for lots of things. I don't know . . .

Uncomfortable with student/teacher relations, Rebecca indignantly summarized the way some students treat teachers:

> The teachers, oh the kids take advantage. Especially the substitute, they'll take advantages, so the teacher will tell you to stop and you won't listen cuz you know that they can't do nothing, cuz they're not strict. So you just keep doing it. So the substitute has to call the proctor and they take them away. I don't know what they do with them then, when they take them away. They probably give them detention.

Rebecca was in Saturday School because of frequent lateness due to responsibilities at home. She described a typical morning of trying to prepare herself and her 5-year-old brother for school:

> . . . it's around seven when I tell him to wake up. Sometimes he'll wake up, but then he'll just open his eyes sometimes, and go back to sleep. Cuz when I tell him to wake up, I go to my room and change, so when I come back out, he should be awake already. But sometimes he's not awake, so I have to keep waking him up. And then, when he's trying to wake up, I go make his lunch, but right after, . . . sometimes he won't cooperate with me, he won't. So I tell him, "Hurry up and get dressed." But he won't help me, get him undressed, put on, you know, pick up his pajamas, he won't help me. . . . it's like dressing a dummy, he's like a little doll or something. It's really hard. So, you know, it takes me a long time to get him dressed. Then, later, I have to go and wash his teeth. He does not want to wash his teeth. So I have to force him to get his teeth washed. And then he does not want me to wash his face, so I have to hold him by forcing him to wash his face, and he starts crying and all that stuff. And I get really frustrated. And then I just start, I just leave him there . . . by himself, and then I go do something else . . . Then after that I have to brush his hair; he does not want me to brush his hair; he won't let me. Then I have to clean his, you know, boogers from his nose; he does not let me do that either. You know, cuz I have to get him clean. Then I have to walk him across the street to the babysitter's house, and that's it.

. . . but, I have like one minute or two minutes that I passed in my time. He delays me like two minutes. But it takes me like a certain amount of time to get here. From my house to here it takes me around ten minutes. And if I walk fast, it takes me ten minutes, walking fast or running. So if I know I'm gonna be two minutes late, I just, you know, I don't, I just say forget it. And I just stay for the whole hour at my house.

. . . Cuz they won't excuse me. Just one little second and my first period teacher, if you're not inside of the room when the bell rings, you're not getting in. Because the other day once, I tried to get, the bell rang and I was one foot away from being inside the door. And he goes, "Nope, you're not going in here." So I had to, you know, go and . . . If I know I'm gonna be like one second late, like forget it, I'm not gonna go anyway.

(*What's your grade like in there?*) Oh, it's terrible. I haven't done anything yet. I haven't been there for a week. I've missed his class for a whole week. I haven't been in there for a long time!

(*Do you think you're gonna pass it?*) I don't know. Right now they're reading, so they're not doing any work. They're reading another book. But I'm gonna see if I can get the book at the library, and maybe try to read it myself, everything they already read. (*What's the book?*) Um *Julius Caesar*, the play. It's the play of *Julius Caesar*. . . . But what would be better for me in my English class would be if my teacher would let me have makeup. But my teacher doesn't have any makeup whatsoever, for anything . . . If you're not there, you're not there. If you don't learn it, you don't learn it.

Rebecca was dropped from her English class and took it during summer school. She earned a B for the semester she missed that year. The following year, her little brother continued to challenge her,

> . . . but this time I try hard to move faster. Cuz my first period is also English and he's kind of rough. He goes, "If you're not here, you're gonna fail." Cuz I missed so many days in his class, and I missed so much work I didn't turn in, but he was nice enough to give me a chance to make up the work, so I was happy for that, so now I have a chance for getting a better grade . . .

Rebecca and her friends also received ABC and Saturday School for lateness to class during the day. Besides being late because "your teacher just closes the door and you can't get in," they were also late because they spent their break at the far end of the campus. "They been messing around with the bells and, well, we couldn't hear them." By the time they saw people moving and returned to their classrooms it was too late to arrive on time. When asked if many people were late, she responded, "Well, most of them, there were like six people that were late. To that same class. Cuz they can't hear the bell either. But the teacher doesn't care, cuz she just closes the door, cuz if you're late, you're late."

Additionally, Rebecca and her friends received detentions and suspensions for ditching. She explained:

> Some kids do it cuz they, sometimes they think . . . better to do that than coming to school, cuz they don't want to tolerate the teacher, or they don't want to do any school

work cuz they're really lazy, or sometimes a friend will tell them that there's gonna be a party that day. There's no other chance to go, you'd have to miss school cuz it's during school. So they go all right. And they want to go have fun, rather than go to school, and to work. And, yeah, or they just want to hang out with those friends who are not going to go to school. And, well, sometimes they want to be with their boyfriends . . . and they want to spend the whole day, so they go to some party still and they spend the whole day there.

Once, Rebecca was seen leaving school in a friend's car and was chased down the street by the school police. She felt scared and nervous when she was caught, but was most concerned about her parents' reactions.

School punishments did not affect her, because Rebecca did not believe she had received them because she did something wrong. She had to care for her brother, didn't hear the bell, and so forth. She compared ABC to being grounded, "like you have to go to your room and do nothing. So kids go through it anyway. It doesn't do anything." Although her parents did not believe in grounding her, she observed her friends being grounded, without result. ABC seemed to be the same:

> So you're there in ABC, all you do is just sit there. You can't talk or anything. Well, that doesn't really do anything; it doesn't kill you. Oh yeah. But you know, when they come back in here, it's like. "Oh wow, I'm going back to ABC, oh well." They don't really care.

Saturday School was a mild deterrent because it is such a waste of time. She added that students who fight are not going to change because of detention because fighting has nothing to do with school work, it "comes out of their own self or something." At best, they might take their fight off campus, but they wouldn't change. Why, she wondered, did the school continue these policies?

Rebecca wants to do well in school and indeed has demonstrated her ability to do acceptable work. The requirements of her family cause some of her problems, but her friends also lead her into difficult situations. What should Rebecca do? Should she change her friends? What can she do about her family? Can the school do anything to help her? Is it the school's responsibility? To what extent should the schools adapt to nonacademic needs? Why?

Stephanie

Stephanie is a European American transfer student in special education classes. When asked to describe herself to the readers she said:

> Well, I'd tell them I'm, you know, give them a fake name, like Stephanie, and give them my age, I'm 18, I'm in tenth grade right now; I'll be in eleventh next year, I live with my parents. I got a job. And . . . I live in a house, not an apartment or anything; I live in a house . . . I *love* school. You know, the only thing I don't like about the schools is they have horrible mouths. Oh, I've had a lot of good friends in the school,

you know, like Fred and some other people. But otherwise . . . I like to learn. It's my priority to learn.

Stephanie wanted to participate in cleaning the campus and painting murals on the walls. She explained, "The reason that's important is because you don't want a messy school. . . . You want your school to look nice. Proper, you know. Most schools don't have nice rooms or anything like that."

Stephanie said the rules here were similar to her previous school, but stricter. This strictness, she believed, was necessary to maintain order on the CHS campus.

Stephanie was going to class when "the proctor kind of caught me on the time." Fooling around with friends had made her late to class for the first time. This was her first detention and she planned to avoid a repetition. She explained:

> It stopped me. I'm not, cuz I learned from it that I shouldn't go back in that place again. (*How did it make you feel in there?*)
>
> It made me feel kind of hurt. I've never done that before. I've had detention before, but not in this school. But otherwise it was too boring for me. I couldn't stand it. When I get bored, I just want to walk out.

In spite of her personal reaction, she maintained, "All I know, detention, Saturday School, ABC, it ain't working [for most students]. It's just useless."

All Stephanie wants to do is fit in with the norm she sees. She carefully considers what behaviors are most effective and attempts to duplicate them. What does special education teach her? What kind of citizen will Stephanie be? What kind of individual? Why do you think so?

Tom

Tom came to the United States from Cambodia before he started school. At age 17, he is combining eleventh- and twelfth-grade general education classes to graduate during the current school year. He says:

> I work at McDonald's. . . . If I have the money, or my family, I'll just start a business right after high school. . . . Probably want to start a business and go to school at the same time. . . . How I act at school . . . I don't know, I'm like half, half. I'm kind of like a student and the other side, like, it's like, well, a friendly guy very friendly to other people, I mean like, my fellow classmates. You know, like a regular student . . . Just one of the guys, just want to have fun, when you have time, you know.

Perhaps because his philosophy included more control than the other students I talked with, Tom was especially aware of the security policies on campus.

> I don't know, it looks like every, like, most of the years, I think it's getting worser and worser. They make the school real strict now. More stricter and stricter, now they have more security. They didn't have that much security . . . when I was first year in CHS.

Tom, who described himself as "a late kind of person," made a special effort to be prompt to all of his classes, but complained that, "In some classes, you go in there, in five minutes, they haven't even done nothing." He added that his teachers don't usually really get to work for ten minutes. He pointed out, however, that attendance was usually taken within the first five minutes and that it was important to have an accurate student count. Tom believed that the new tardy policy was instituted because the administration was afraid that students would just extend their lateness and ditch the whole period. He felt they thought punishing students for being tardy might make them think twice the next time and not do it again.

Tom had been officially disciplined twice, both times for leaving campus. In the previous year he was caught going out to lunch, but this time he was late returning to school from an appointment. His mother was unable to talk with the disciplinarian until after the paperwork was done, so he was assigned Saturday School. Although his mother tried to clear the matter up several times, she was unable to do so. Finally, she suggested that it would be easier for her son to just go ahead and go to Saturday School. Tom was very indignant about the way his mother was treated by the administration.

Saturday School was a punishment for Tom because he had to miss a picnic he had wanted to attend. He wanted to avoid being assigned detentions in the future.

Tom wants to be a successful "American" but sometimes resents what he has to put up with. His mother encourages him to fit in without making a fuss. His plans are ambitious, but he also seems very relaxed. What is Tom learning about citizenship? What do you think students should learn? Why?

Tracy

Tracy is an African American general education tenth grader. Her strong opinions are rooted in thoughtful reactions to her observations of the world, her outspoken behaviors leavened by humor. When interactions with others conflict with her self-respect, she stands up for herself in spite of possible negative outcomes.

Tracy received frequent detention assignments, but she never believed they were earned. First, she talked about a girl she knows who is constantly in trouble for "stealing and stuff" on campus as being truly deserving of detention. Her own "misbehaviors" were not worth the fuss. More importantly, detentions were unfairly assigned.

Many students, although concerned about being dropped from a class for multiple tardies, or worried about missing work because they were excluded from the period, were also very annoyed about their treatment. Tracy observed angrily, ". . . they be like a few, a second, a minute late, they'll slam the door in your face." When asked why there is a rule about being in class on time, she responded,

> They make like so they don't miss anything, the teachers say. But the teachers, all they do at the beginning is gripe. Gripe, gripe, gripe, gripe. . . . (*What would be a good*

way for the teachers to start class?) Not griping! . . . Just not gripe. . . . "Get your homework out. Everyone who didn't do it, got detention . . ."

Tracy believed that social discussions were important and enjoyed being permitted to talk in some classes. Sometimes, however, the rules were unclear, and students got yelled at for talking after they had been told they could. She also wondered how it was that only one person (usually her) was punished for an activity that required at least two people to perform.

> You can't just talk to yourself, unless I'm going crazy . . . So I don't see how he can just single out one person and just give them detention, and not give the other person detention that they was talking to, or that was talking to them.

She had received about sixteen afterschool detentions from this teacher and was assigned Saturday School when she did not attend them. Her reaction to this teacher generally led to more trouble:

> Cuz I figure if I'm going to get in trouble, I'm gonna annoy him as much as I can. I'm already going to get in trouble, he deserve it, if he gonna keep singling me out, so I get on his nerves! . . . If you know you're already getting in trouble, why shut up? . . . He sits up there and threatens me like I supposed to get scared. I was real, "Ooooooh, wow . . ." I be messin' with him, be like, "Oh, I'm really scared." And everybody start laughin' because I be messing with him. Because he'll mess with me first. I don't be doing that. But you know, like someone telling me something, "Why you talking, Tracy?" "I'm just listening! Dang! Leave me alone!"

Tracy said her teacher claimed that her group was too loud. She maintained that the other group was at least as noisy and implied that his evaluation of the class' noise level was a result of another instance of unfair treatment by the teacher:

> . . . He won't play the radio for us. . . . He claims we talk too much! If the radio was on people wouldn't be talking, they'd be listening to the music. But no, "I would try to be quiet before I put the radio in there." But my friend had walked into (the same teacher's previous) class and they was all noisy, and the radio was still on.

Tracy was accused of "throwing the discus around the room" because she tripped over a boy's foot and the computer disk flew out of her hand. She was also accused of defiance and dropped from ROTC when she refused to accede to the teacher's demand that she do fifty pushups a day. She expected teachers to make their expectations clear and reasonable. Thus, when she was scheduled for an afterschool detention four or five days in the future, she felt she should have been be reminded of the assignment on the detention day. Instead, she forgot to attend and received another Saturday School assignment.

When asked why she was in Saturday School this week, Tracy answered, "They claim it's for defiance,[5] but I don't agree." Tracy argued with a teacher who disciplined her unfairly; she wouldn't allow his misperceptions to pass without comment:

> No, I be cool. I be being quiet. But he like, keep like messing with me. Like one time, he just made me mad . . . I had to tell him something. Because I'm like, we was up in the class, right, and he kept yelling at us, "Stop talking!"
>
> I was like, "I ain't talking. I'm just gonna sit here, for like ten minutes. These Hispanic girls behind us, they was just going off talking." He didn't say a thing to me. He didn't say a thing to them. I was, like, "Hold up. Excuse me, Mr. Teacher." I said, "How come they can talk and we can't?"
>
> "Well, I couldn't hear them."
>
> "You couldn't hear them, but I'm sitting in front of them." And his desk is like three inches away from ours. And I'm like, "You can't hear them, but they right in my ear, and I can hear 'em . . . I know their whole conversation and what they was talking about. That's annoying me, but I can't talk." . . . I was like, "That ain't right. You don't never say nothing to them when they talking, but as soon as we open our mouth, you start jumping all over us."
>
> "Uh, I didn't hear them."
>
> "Get a hearing aid. Turn up your Miracle Ear. Cuz everybody heard them talking. Everybody could tell you what they was talking about."
>
> "I didn't hear them."
>
> But as soon as *we* talk, he hears *us*.

Tracy thought that ABC was boring ("They make you just sit there and *look at the wall!*"), but Saturday School was fun. "They won't give you ABC if you ask for Saturday School," so she usually went to Saturday School. She said that detentions weren't going to change her behavior, although they did make her mad sometimes. She added that although detention was designed to be a deterrent for certain behaviors, it was actually an incentive to find ways to circumvent the rules.

Tracy is extremely intelligent, but placed in general education classes. She has learned to live in a system that she finds to be uncomfortable and dishonest. What is Tracy learning in school? What future do you predict for her? Why?

Some Conclusions

Most students had been late to class. Some received Saturday School or ABC for leaving school without permission, or "ditching." Others had problems with class

---

[5]Insubordination and defiance are loosely defined. They indicate refusal to submit, or resistance to authority, as demonstrated by behavior that goes beyond talking back to blatant disobedience in attitude, speech, or action. Students who received a Saturday School assignment for "insubordination" or "defiance" were generally still angry about it. They felt their reactions were justified and that the teacher was unfair.

behavior, especially talking. All of the students had observed and most admitted to talking in class, but condemned disrespect to teachers. Several said that they or a friend had been disciplined for fighting on campus. Others spoke of acts that administrators categorized as defiance or insubordination, although the students did not agree with this label when applied to themselves. Generally, then, students were assigned detention at City High School for the same reasons that students receive detention throughout the United States. But are their reactions the same across the country?

In spite of contradictions, self-censorship, and attempts to tell me what they thought I wanted to hear, it seems clear that these students do not share the values being enforced by the school.

No student mentioned tardiness or ditching as behavior problems. They thought tardiness was sometimes necessary; catching up was the student's responsibility. Ditching was not desirable, but occasionally acceptable, either to avoid punishment for tardiness or to alleviate boredom. Again, it was the student's responsibility to attend class and to make up for any missed work. How can we reconcile these diverse points of view? Or should we?

Almost all of the students agreed that there was a lack of respect, both for adults and fellow students on campus. Instead of developing respectful behavior, the current discipline system often reinforces adults' disrespectful interactions with students and parents. Although they complained of others' lack of respect, the students did not seem to question their own behavior. Should they? Is "respect" an academic issue? How do schools define respect?

Several students were also concerned with a lack of safety for themselves and their property. An intricate system of city police, campus police, and proctors seemed ineffective. How do school experiences affect students' understanding of the larger community?

Special and general education students complained about course content. Other researchers suggest that this is a common reaction and that students cope with boredom and irrelevance in classes through substance use, outside diversions, and rebellious responses or disobedience to rules. Could curriculum be a cause for discipline problems? Should it be changed to reflect the wishes of the students? Are students able to make decisions about their adult needs?

Several studies found high school students do not see agreement or consistency within the school when specific infractions are punished. Casper, Johnny, Tracy, and Carla used nonstandard American English and made references to a lower socioeconomic system. Tom, Alissa, and Angela demonstrated clear middle class behaviors and goals. Is discipline really a class issue rather than a justice issue?

Both at CHS and nationally, some students are unaware of the rules or their consequences. They feel their participation in the process is minimal, and that the school's rules are inherently unfair and inconsistently enforced. Some students are dissatisfied and cynical about the system and openly state their intention to continue breaking rules. The current discipline system is not improving their behavior—is it contributing to misbehavior?

As their goals and aspirations are rejected by the school culture, so do adolescents reject the institution's values and the adults who impose them (Finifter, 1972). Hollingsworth, Lufler, and Clune (1984) maintain that the profile of a troublemaker includes future plans that do not relate well to a lifelong goal. They also suggest that the troublemaker role is a part of the student's personal identification.[6]

What rules are we enforcing? What behaviors are we trying to develop? What reactions are actually occurring? What effects do traditional discipline procedures have on learning, living, and becoming adults?

---

[6]Review Michelle Fine's work on tracking and dropouts for more current, but consistent, observations about troublemakers.

2

Controlling Students' Behavior

But it seems that the kids keep control in the class and the teachers don't . . .

—Carla

Although treated separately, educational indices include three areas under the heading of "discipline": physical, intellectual, and spiritual. Originally, they were united in concept, thus explaining some common assumptions about the relationships of consequence to future behavior: Hitting a student (physical discipline) will improve learning (intellectual discipline); memorizing scripture (intellectual discipline) will improve morality (spiritual discipline). Because physically punishing behavior is assumed to influence intellectual and moral understanding, keeping a child after school is also expected to eliminate unrelated behaviors. The concept of "discipline" is closely intertwined with both academic study, when we refer to specific areas of study, and punitive treatment.[1]

School discipline policies usually reflect the assumption that deviant behavior is undesirable and can be eradicated by punitive consequences. Like the ancient Egyptians, schools in the United States use repetition and exactitude in designing an education to replicate traditional society. Theories of behavior and its control are developed to meet these ends, often continuing to assume that punishment is the best way to eliminate deviance and enforce unquestioning acceptance.

---

[1]Butts' multiple histories (1947, 1955, 1973) of education are my main source of information about the development of discipline theory as seen in most public schools in the United States.

Rules

> *They've got rules for everything you do.*
>
> —Chaquan

Whether in general or special education, controlling students is a part of the teacher's job. The law has assigned us parental responsibilities for the safety of students and judicial obligations to protect their constitutional rights.[2] In order to teach, we must demand student attention or expect students to accomplish specific tasks in order to complete or enhance the learning experience. In an emergency, we are trained in procedures to evacuate students from a building; they are expected to follow teacher direction. Traditionally, we have used punishments, such as detention, and rewards, such as grades, to maintain that control.

Gathercoal (1998) suggests that rules and consequences be considered as a parallel to the Bill of Rights. Students' rights as individuals must be balanced by their responsibilities as students. School rules, used to communicate those responsibilities, are equated to laws, which should be "fair and reasonable." Justice in both courts and schools is partially protected by due process procedures.

When I started teaching, I expected good behavior, as defined by my parents and schoolteachers, from my students. This behavior had enabled me to succeed in school, so I thought it was a requirement for successful learning. My colleagues and most public schools had similar standards. If these standards weren't met, I became angry. Schools had lists of expected behaviors that were even stricter than mine. If administrators became aware of infractions of their standards, they became angry and had lists of punishments they could mete out for each misdemeanor. Teachers believed that they should solve problems within the classroom, because too many referrals were frowned upon by the administration.

Common Sense Rules

Although we often assume school standards to be the result of common sense, it is important to understand that common sense is a product of common culture. Students bring a variety of ideas of common sense and assumptions about standards to the school environment. In order to avoid confusion about what is required by the school versus what is taught at home or learned in the street, schools and teachers establish explicit rules.

In my class, I assumed that students should pay attention to me and the class activities above anything else. They were taught at home to greet friends and relatives by name whenever they saw someone they knew. Thus, when we left the

---

[2]Gathercoal (1998) notes that current court decisions support student rights unless the school rules or procedures protect property, educational purpose, health and safety, or educational process. He further states, "Educators have no constitutional rights in the student-educator relationship. Their rights exist only through the employer-employee relationship." (p. 201)

door open on a hot day, class discussions, presentations, and lectures were often punctuated by shouted greetings to and from people walking through the hall. Additionally, street wisdom suggested that individuals from certain neighborhoods be greeted with an insult designed to lead to confrontation. The complications were endless and most easily solved by my caveat, "No talking to people in the hall!" Mistake number one.

Effective Rules

Negative rules are not very efficient. They do not give the student a clear cue of what behaviors are expected, so students from different backgrounds may have to experiment with other options before discovering the correct response. Some students may use the rule as an excuse for other unacceptable actions. "No running in the halls" enables students to argue the permissibility of hopping, skipping, cartwheeling, fighting, and so forth. Your choice is to make a rule for every behavior you don't want to see or to make a rule for the behavior you do want to see. The rule "Walk in the halls" means you can legitimately stop a student from running, prevent lingering by lockers, and disperse congregations in crowded areas by citing the positive rule.

Sometimes rules are made in response to a specific, unimagined situation. Clothing styles and social mores change constantly and unpredictably. New rules are one way to react to an unexpected, unacceptable situation. As these rules are no longer needed, they fall by the wayside, but are still enforceable. Eventually it becomes difficult to remember all of the rules, especially if you didn't look at them in the first place. Three to five broad rules are easy to remember and monitor. Well-constructed rules designed to keep the classroom running smoothly will encompass unexpected behaviors.[3]

Imposed rules are part of life, but also very frustrating. My first reaction is to ignore or circumvent them. If I have a say in the establishment of a rule, as I theoretically do in a democratic society, I am more likely to obey it. If I understand (and agree with) the rationale for a law, I am more comfortable with following it. The same is true of teenagers. Sandra Schaal, a teacher in my school, used an activity she found to be effective in establishing and enforcing rules. First, she asked the students to list the behaviors essential for being a good student. She listed the ideas on the board as they brainstormed and then helped them combine and generalize until they reduced the list to three to five rules. The discussion helped the students examine their academic behaviors and share specific examples of abstractions such as "respect." Then they repeated the activity to create a list of rules for the teacher. Again, they began to make observations about learning and successful academic

---

[3]My rules are:
    Respect others
    Do your work
    Pamper the teacher
What are yours?

Rules for Rules

Culturally appropriate—Good rules reflect the culture of the class: They honor the values of the students and the teachers and lead to effective learning behaviors.

Positive—Good rules tell participants what they should be doing.

Few in number—Three to five general rules are more manageable than many specific rules.

Designed by students—Rules are more highly valued if all participants have a role in designing them.

Clear behaviors—Standards should either be observable and measurable (sit at your own desk) or, if abstract (respect others), discussed and role played.

environments. The rules were posted for several weeks, then revised and put on posters, which were displayed and referred to throughout the year.

Hansen and Childs (1998) suggest some rules may be rooted in tradition, ritual, and history. Those that encourage and permit rather than restrict and direct are more likely to promote effective schooling, which must allow for risk-taking experiences.

Rules and consequences must be clear to students; substitutes, administrators, and parents should also be notified of them. A few students may need a structured warning procedure, but others will learn that a warning procedure means opportunities to misbehave before being punished. Yet, it is important to be fair and consistent with enforcement. Private agreements about systems of enforcement help students understand apparent inconsistencies.

The Students' Experiences

The transfer students, Casper and Stephanie, knew they had to find out about the rules in their new school to avoid getting in trouble. When students I talked to broke a specific rule, they knew it and disagreed with the rule itself rather than the punishment.

Misbehavior in class was the most hotly contested infraction because there did not seem to be specific rules or consistent consequences. The teacher could assign an afterschool detention in the classroom or write an office referral. The office could assign a Saturday School; send the student to in-school suspension in the ABC Room, either for that class or for the rest of the day; require the student to stay in the office for the period; or any combination of these consequences. Parents were usually, but not always, notified of office referrals.

Talking. Students were often reprimanded for talking in class. Some received Saturday School either as a result of talking or of missing teacher detentions assigned for talking. They complained of observing other students who talked without being punished. All of the students recognized the importance of listening when the teacher talked and agreed that there should be silence during a test. They agreed that talking should not be allowed to interfere with a learning activity, but believed it to be acceptable as a parallel activity and to actually enhance learning at times.

Several students valued explanations and help offered by their peers in class. Angela explained, "You get other, different opinions, you get different facts, and if you don't know how to do something, like other people that you're working with might know."

It was also rewarding to assist classmates. Stephanie told proudly of helping another student learn to use the dictionary. Don spoke of sharing information about activities in other classes, valuable reminders to do specific tasks, and challenges to surpass others, but pointed out that when he really wants to get work done, he needs to focus on the task and not listen to his friends' talk. Johnny added that it also helped when he was reminded by his friends to stop talking. The students resented being reprimanded or punished for helping their peers.

Several students also brought up the role of social talk in the classroom. Again, Angela explained:

> I know some people if something really interesting happens, and they weren't allowed to talk about it, they'd probably be thinking what happened and they wouldn't do what they're supposed to do. . . . It's just like you're going to keep them in suspense all that time; they're not really going to be paying attention to their work. And that's all they're gonna think about is what happened at lunch . . . Tell them and get it out of the way.

Tracy agreed that social discussions were important. She enjoyed being permitted to talk in some classes, but sometimes got yelled at for talking after she had been told she could. She also wondered why only one person (usually her) was punished for an activity that required at least two people to perform. She was told that her group was too loud, but she did not believe that to be true. She was sure that the previous class was louder than hers, but they still were able to talk and listen to the radio.

Chaquan had a teacher who favored one side of the room over another. "Blacks, Mexicans that sit on this side and Whites, Mexicans that sit over there and some Chinese people and she don't never say nothing to them."

Respect. Showing respect was another behavior some students were working on. They all seemed to have a clear understanding of respect versus disrespect, and they all wanted to be in a respectful environment, but couldn't always manage it. Carla wanted to be respectful to her teacher, but thought the teacher was forcing her into an embarassing situation. As we conversed, she expressed a pessimistic view of students' attitudes:

Rude to their teacher? Well, sometimes it's not right, but, like, you know, they should not . . . They should respect the teacher, like the teacher should respect the kids. But sometimes, you know, the kids have attitudes, they'll start yelling. But it seems that the kids keep control in the class and the teachers don't . . . well, they'll do something, but they don't care. The kids don't care. (*What do we do about those kids who don't care?*) Nothing. It's, that's the way they are . . . Mike dropped out of school because he didn't like the classes. He didn't learn nothing. And he would just walk out and they would give him a referral and everything, but he didn't care. It seems like, you know . . .

Tracy said she did not believe being rude to a teacher was appropriate behavior but, "They're gonna do what they want. And I'm gonna do what I'm gonna do."

Several students said they were accused of talking back when they were actually trying to clarify a situation or defend themselves. Casper explained, "You can't really argue with them, because then they'll put another check on your name, and say, 'You're arguing with the teacher.'" He continued:

There've been times when I've tried to explain myself to a teacher and she says I'm giving a hard, like one time she was going to refer me to the office, and I said, "I don't want to be referred, can I explain you something?" Then she wrote on the referral that I was giving her a hard time refusing to go to the office and stuff. And so I was just trying to talk to her to see if I could get another chance, cuz I didn't do it that time, the kids did it. They were playing; they took my umbrella and I started to get upset, and so she goes, "Everybody sit down." And I was up trying to get my umbrella from them. They were throwing it around the class, always playing around, and she was all, "Casper, didn't I tell you to sit down?" I was all, cuz I wasn't actually doing nothing, so I was like shouting, I was like, "I'm trying to get my umbrella, alright? When I get it, I'll sit down." "That's why I'm referring you." And then I tried to explain myself and she was, "I don't want to hear it. Go to the office."

He repeated, "You can't really argue with the substitute, cuz they're always right, any teacher, really." He tells about being blamed for turning out the lights because he had been out of his seat, throwing something away.

Oh, I got Saturday School for it. . . . And then I tried talking to her calmly, I calmed down, cuz first I started yelling. And I calmed down, I was like, "Can I talk to you?" And she was all mad, "Oh, I don't want to talk to you right now! I don't have time! You guys always do this!" And then I was like, "Oh" (shrugs). And then I'm not gonna snitch on my friends, especially there, cuz then you have problems with them, so I just . . .

I explained that to the principal and it's like, can't really argue with the teacher, then she's just gonna put more on the list.

Attendance.   All of the students could explain the complex rules and consequences for tardiness. If they were outside of the room after the late bell rang, they had to go to the ABC room instead of their class for the period. They then were to meet with the teacher after school for a classroom detention. The third through fifth tardies they also received an office referral and a Saturday School assignment. Their parents were notified about these actions. The sixth lateness resulted in their being dropped from the class and having to make up the credit in summer school or during the following year. If the dropped class occurred at the beginning or the end of the day, they were not to be on campus during that time. If it was in the middle of the day, either their schedule was rearranged or they spent that period in the ABC room.

The students disliked the tardiness rule. They were concerned about missing work because they were excluded or about being dropped from a class and losing the credit. Several students were willing to make up lost time or adjust their schedules, but did not feel they could promise to be in class on time because of other commitments, such as childcare, transportation constraints, or difficulties crossing campus in a timely manner. They knew that teachers were annoyed by delays and disruptions caused by their lateness, but believed that it should be the student's problem. Angela pointed out that it is the student's responsibility to find out what was missed, not the teacher's duty to wait until everyone is present. Chaquan summed up the students' feelings:

> They shouldn't give us referrals and all that for first period, cuz everybody's gonna be late. That's not gonna change. I don't know why they're doing it. It won't change for me.

Others, such as Tracy, were angry about what they perceived to be an arbitrary and vindictive attitude on the teachers' part. She observed, ". . . they be like a few, a second, a minute late, they'll slam the door in your face." Tom resented having to rush to classes and then spend five or ten minutes waiting for the teacher to take attendance, organize papers, and set up equipment.

One of the easiest ways to avoid a referral for tardiness was to leave the school grounds, or ditch. Students could also be referred for ditching if they went to the restroom without a pass from the teacher or were out of the room without a pass during class time. Of course, students often ditched for the entire day, for a number of reasons. They stayed home to avoid a test or due date, watched movies, had friends over, or went window shopping. They often found ditching to be more boring than school. They did not think habitual ditching was desirable, because of the potential loss of credit, but found it to be acceptable, even necessary at times.

Many students left campus for lunch. This was a privilege allowed to seniors with parental permission, but considered to be ditching when younger students did it. Although they argued that the food on campus was not acceptable, the allotted time was too short and the lines were too long, their main concern was the idea of senior privilege as opposed to equal treatment. No student believed that leaving campus for lunch should be punished.

Ditching could also lead students into more serious trouble. They had heard of (but never attended) ditching parties that included substance abuse and indiscriminate sexual activity. Both Ana and Rebecca were returned to school by municipal police when they were caught ditching.

If caught ditching, students could be assigned to Saturday School and/or in-school suspension in the ABC room, depending on the nature and number or classes missed and student's previous record. Parents were notified.

Fighting.   Although all of the students agreed that fighting was against the rules and should be discouraged, those who were caught fighting felt the fight was unavoidable. Teachers and administrators ignored some fights but assigned suspensions or expulsions for others, depending on the severity of the fight. The students who talked about individual fighting seemed to accept physical violence as a part of their lives. They were aware of the school's policy about fighting and were willing to accept Saturday School or suspension when those rules were in conflict with their own priorities.

Johnny told about a big fight he was involved in:

> No, it was during school, it was the first year, the start of school. He [a classmate] thinks he's all bad, and he thinks I'm the one who was beating up on his friend, and he grabbed me, and I said, "What are you grabbing me for, man? I didn't do no shit." And he says, "You beat up my friend." I said, "I did what! I didn't beat up no one." There was more Mexicans in the class than him, so I said, "Hey, I'll beat him up." "Go ahead! Fuck him! Beat the fuck out of him! Man, we'll back you up!" And I told him, "You better not touch me again or I'll kick your ass, I swear. "And he just touched me because . . . one of his friends [told him], "Oh, it's not him, it's not him! He's not the one who beat up on your home boy. That's another guy." So blah, blah. Then I said, "You better not do mistakes again. I'll kick your ass." And then he says, "Yeah, right." And I said, "Wanna go? Wanna go for it now?" And he says, "Yeah, let's go for it." And he says, "Oh." Cuz there was more Mexicans than him, so he was afraid of us. Then another time, another guy, a Mexican socked a Black, in the face, and he let him bleed, and then that's how it started riots too. And then another riot with the Chinese, they just got in, and they started shanking on my friend. They shanked him with a screwdriver and we got mad at the Chinese. Because the Chinese wanted to start, too, with us, too. You know, not just the Blacks, you know.

Although most of students felt it was wrong to start a fight in school, those who fought said they had to return a blow. Tracy explained, "Sometimes you got to fight . . . Sometimes you can't help it. Somebody go up to you; they swing at you, what you gonna do then? Stand there and say, 'I won't fight,' and get beat up?"

Casper talked about trying to avoid a fight in school:

> I got in a fight with this kid in the office, in front of the security guard. I didn't plan it that way. I was in my class and the kid, when he told on me, cuz he was messing with me and he said that, he told on me that I was always messing with him.
>
>   And so I went in the office and he was in the principal's office and I was sitting down, and he was all, like mumbling some stuff and he asked the lady, "Can I go get a drink? Can I go get a drink from the drinking fountain?"
>
>   The lady said, "Yeah." He walked by me, he started to, he like said something. I ignored him, then he came back in and he got in my face and so I stood up and he started talking and then he pushed me back, so I pushed him and he tried swinging

and he hit me in the side of the head. And then I hit him in his face and the security guard jumped over and I almost hit the security guard . . . The kid pushed me, then he swung at me. *Then* I hit him . . . Cuz then everybody in the school would be like, "You didn't swing back," . . . even my mom said, "After the first swing, don't stand there."

Casper also thought it important to fight one on one, but size doesn't matter. He said,

I could go up to a seventh . . . grader, he could be smaller than me and still beat me. Or I could go up to a twelfth grader, it doesn't mean the size, it's how you fight and stuff. And I don't mean to fight and stuff, but if I have to, I'll defend myself.

Carla tried to avoid a fight, but her friends literally pushed her into one:

. . . She was teasing me, you know, "Yeah, I have a boyfriend," and everything. And that day she was walking and she was talking about me, and I was gonna push her, but then I went "No," and my friend pushed me into her. And then she turned around and she was gonna sock me and I just started fighting with her . . . She turned around and she swanged at me. And I went back, you know. I had to do something. And I fought with her.

Johnny was willing to initiate a fight if he was "bothered by others." He had, for example, been given Saturday School for kicking another student, who said things about his mother.

Many students agreed with Angela who said,

I don't even go to fights. Like when people say there's a fight, I just stay where I am, cuz I know by the time you get there, first of all, it's gonna be over, cuz you attract attention and the proctors come, and they break it up. So, why do you have to go watch a fight when you know it's gonna be over by the time you get there. And then you just instigated more when you go around there.

A Teacher's Reaction

As a beginning teacher, I did a lot of criticizing of student behavior and student work. I assumed that my comments would lead to improvements, and sometimes they did. I also "yelled" at kids, scolding them harshly, without particularly raising my voice, and sent incorrigible students to the office, where something happened to them. "Good" administrators caused them to change their behavior with some sort of punishment; "bad" administrators "talked to them" but did not affect their behavior.

The faculty room echoed with our complaints and righteous anger. Where did it come from?

Punishment

A Brief History of Punishment in Education

Usually translated as "instruction," the Hebrew word *musar* also means "chastisement" and "discipline" (Brubaker, 1947). The book of Proverbs (circa 900 B.C.E.) uses the work *musar* thirty times, including the original version of the saying "Spare the rod and spoil the child." Ancient Jewish teachers were advised, in a variety of sources, to punish all wrongdoing (Barclay, 1959). Greek, Roman, and medieval monks usually punished their students harshly, but there were always those who disagreed with the practice. The argument continues in modern homes and schools.

Theology strongly affected the policies implemented in colonial New England schools. Besides emphasizing memorization of rules and texts, European Reformation schools developed other procedures that were carried across the Atlantic, including standardization, grading, prescribed curriculum, mandatory attendance, and requirements for passing into the next grade. Strict rules forbade fighting, carrying weapons, cheating, lying, gambling, swearing, dicing, card playing, swimming, skating, and bird catching. Deviation from these rules could be punished by whipping, ridicule, and the use of a dunce's cap or dullard's stool (Butts, 1947).

Since colonial times, schools in the United States have experienced violence from the students, teachers, and administrators. John Cotton, a Puritan leader, suggested a discipline plan that included whippings, lectures, and sermons, with death for otherwise incorrigible students (Butts, 1955). In 1837, even whips could not control the Massachusetts students who drove 300 teachers out of the school (Lightfoot, 1983).

Detention, corporal punishment, and suspension are the traditional punishments that continue to be used in public schools (Mansfield & Farris, 1992). Physical punishment seems to effectively reduce deviant behaviors in the schools, although it raises ethical questions (Millman, Schaefer, & Cohen, 1980), so even liberal programs often include strict rules and punitive measures to control violent students and establish a safe environment. Principals of schools that serve students from lower socioeconomic neighborhoods strongly assert their need for power to institute changes in student behavior. They believe that underachieving students must be disciplined and mannerly before they can learn (Lightfoot, 1983).

Current Practice

Behaviorists have analyzed the observable effects of punishment according to their definition: "a consequence of behavior which reduces the future probability of that behavior or as an operation in which an aversive stimulus is made contingent upon a response" (O'Leary & O'Leary, 1972, p. 151). Behavior is most effectively reduced by withdrawing a reinforcement. Aversive stimuli result in the disappearance of the undesirable behavior, but the change may be only temporary (Patterson, 1977).

Skinner also believed that the punished behavior would be likely to reappear when the punishment was removed (Hergenhahn, 1976).

Research indicates that punishment can suppress or weaken behavior, but its effectiveness is closely related to timing, available responses, and the relationships of the people involved. Further, it seems ancient Greek educators were correct in their belief that punishment should be sparing to avoid negative side effects. To be effective, the reason should be clear to the student, there should be a complementary positive reinforcement for desired behavior, physical punishment should be avoided, punishment should not be administered in anger, and punishment should occur at the initiation of the behavior (Hergenhahn, 1976; O'Leary & O'Leary, 1972).

A Teacher's Response

Punishment does stop behaviors when properly administered, and there are some behaviors, such as bringing a weapon to school or throwing a sharp object across the room, which I don't think should be repeated. Also, we don't get "blank slates" in secondary schools. Students come to us with existing concepts of behavior and consequences. Those who have been schooled in a negative environment may not respond to praise or counseling. "I'd rather you not do that," is meaningless to a student who understands that adults aren't serious until voice and fist are raised. While they learn other ways to interact, some punishment may be necessary to control their inappropriate, disruptive, or dangerous behaviors.[4]

Also, I'm sorry to say, sometimes I needed revenge. I can only take so much, and then I get really angry. I want someone to suffer. Granted, I don't feel as great as I expected after I cream some kid, but there is a certain regrettable satisfaction. Sandra Schaal, a social studies teacher, much more even tempered than I, told her students about her limited supply of "nice." First period students were fortunate, because they came to class when she had a full supply of nice available. By seventh period, however, students would be wise to evaluate her mood carefully, because she sometimes ran out of niceness. Her students began to notice which periods used up more nice than others and became more aware of effective social interactions.

Understanding my own temper and temperament was important for two reasons. First, knowing my own personality traits enabled me to control and use them to the best advantage. Second, in moments of honest reflection, I caught myself blaming the students for my imperfections. Understanding my role in interactions helped me solve many problems and avoid others.

---

[4]Other teachers agree. Kreisberg (1990) discovered that teachers believe they need to use discipline *on* students before they can work *with* them. Some students will not respond to anything but punishment, which has been shown to reduce aggression, perhaps because penalties increase the student's attention and caution, while rewards distract the student from the task and increase impulsive behavior (Millman et al., 1980).

Analyzing my own behavior helped me learn about my personal warning signs. If I lost my temper with an individual, no matter what punishment was meted out, the student won. Getting a teacher to turn red in the face, sputter, or otherwise lose self-control is a big victory for the student. If I acted before I lost control, I could act angry enough to convince the class of my anger,[5] but speak and behave in an effective, responsible manner. I could scold coherently and fluently (one kid gave me a standing ovation for a tirade; he said I could yell at him better than his mother) and come up with creative, humorous reactions or consequences. When I expressed anger and frustration honestly and openly, students reacted. They did not like me to be angry with them so they either changed their behavior or discussed it with me while I was still able to converse coherently. They also liked to avoid my tirades, so they warned each other about pushing the limits, sometimes even before I was annoyed.

Awareness of my temper was part of a giant step forward in my teaching: Admitting to imperfections relieved me of the need to be perfect. I no longer needed to blame others for my difficulties, nor did I need to beat myself up about them. I didn't have to hide behind euphemisms or excuses. Instead of blaming a student for "choosing" to misbehave, I could wonder what choices the student had. Did he "choose" to sleep in class and work late in order to buy a prom ticket or food for the family? Did she "choose" to crack jokes rather than expire of boredom in a dull class? Did they "choose" to reject the work I gave them because they had done it for the past four years or because it was completely irrelevant to their needs? Did they "choose" to misbehave for a reason we could examine, or were they just trying to agitate me?

Consequences

Admitting to my desire for revenge yanked the curtain from the euphemism of "consequence."[6] A natural consequence is the result of a behavior without outside manipulation. Natural consequences are wonderful teaching tools, but often very inconvenient in the classroom. When a student misuses equipment, the consequence is damage to the equipment, or the child. If I did something as a result of the behavior, it was a reaction, a punishment or reward, not a natural consequence. The natural consequence of being late to class is not detention, but missing whatever happened in class. If all that happens is roll call and criticism of previous work, maybe lateness is the more intelligent choice. Sometimes I had to look at my practice in order to change student behavior.

Gathercoal's (1998) Judicious Consequences are not designed to punish or reward, but rather to assist students as they develop attitudes of respect and responsibility necessary for a democratic community.

---

[5]If I was cool, calm, and ladylike, my students didn't believe I was really angry, so I did have to emote a little.

[6]I don't like using euphemisms for punishments, but Skiba and Deno (1991) posit that because punishment is effective, it should be used, but the terminology should be exchanged for a more emotionally neutral vocabulary.

Effective Punishment

If you believe in revenge, or quid pro quo suffering, an effective punishment is a reaction that causes the miscreant to suffer to the same or greater degree as the behavior caused others to suffer. This can be a good thing for your own mental health or to support a sense of fairness in the classroom, but it is difficult to measure the correct portions of suffering. If your purpose is to eliminate an undesirable behavior in a student or group, an effective punishment is whatever consequence causes the behavior to disappear. The type and severity of effective consequences vary with the students and their individual and collective priorities.

After identifying your goals, you must choose some punishments. With the exception of such consequences as electric shock, loud noise, or decapitation (all leading to worse consequences for the teacher than for the student), no punishment is universal. Some students are devastated by a raised eyebrow or quiet correction, others pride themselves on being unmoved by anything less than consequences that far exceed what the original behavior calls for. Even chocolate can be a punishment for some students, while others actually enjoy sucking on a lemon.

You need to plan punitive discipline in advance, because you will not have time to think things out when you are in the middle of a situation.

Adversive stimuli, such as physical punishments, generally cause some sort of pain. They are great for revenge, but do have complex side effects. If you want to punish with adversive stimuli, you need to do it immediately and consistently to extinguish a specific behavior, because the brain makes a subconscious connection with the behavior and the consequence. Thus, we learn not to touch a stove after we are burned or not to fall asleep in class when an ice cube is placed on our neck. This can be problematic in the classroom, because you have to be constantly on the alert for the misbehavior. You must punish talking immediately so that the student does not associate the smack on the head with doing his or her worksheet.[7] Fortunately, most students have the cognitive capacity to relate a consequence to an earlier behavior, although the more time that elapses between the two, the weaker the connection.

Response-cost procedures are methods of punishment that remove a previously earned or expected reward. Misbehavior may result in removal of points, tokens, or free time. It can be used successfully with individuals or groups. An immediate response-cost might be the removal of the student from the group or the room, which is punishing for some students, rewarding for others. When used as punishment, it is referred to as "kicking the kid out." When used as a time for quiet reflection, before a consequence is decided upon, it is referred to as "time-out."

Time-out is most valuable when you and the student need some space to cool down. It is useful to have a secluded but observable place in the room. An exchange agreement with a neighboring teacher can also provide a good time-out location. I

---

[7]You should not use physical punishment in the classroom for many reasons, including liability issues. Parental permission is not reliable. Schools that include corporal punishment in their discipline codes generally delineate a specific procedure and administrator, who is often not the teacher. The importance of following this procedure *to the letter* is another reason for acting before you lose control of your temper.

used the office as a time-out location, but that sometimes resulted in conflict or miscommunication with the school disciplinarians. Remember, the student gets time-out, not the teacher; and don't send a misbehaver to an air-conditioned space when your room is hot.

It is also important to consider legal and ethical issues when planning and implementing severe punitive discipline procedures. Generally, they should be used as a last resort, with previous incidents of the behavior and the consequences well documented. It may be wise to inform the parents of planned punishments so that communication problems can be avoided.

Some Successes

My instructional aides and I found that the most effective punishments were private (generally after school) and at least slightly humorous. We satisfied our immature needs for revenge, and the behavior usually disappeared.

Talkers were invited to come in after school. Applying the theory that satiation decreases behavior, we let them leave as soon as they had talked without stopping for ten minutes. An alternative was to require ten consecutive minutes of silence. In the ninth minute, we would have someone come in the room and greet the student. Politeness and training demanded a response and earned the student another ten minutes.

Every so often we had a rash of whistlers. They could come in after school, eat a package of soda crackers, and leave as soon as they could whistle a verse of a popular song.

Throwing is a particular peeve of mine. We cut up a half dozen tissues into two-inch squares and allowed the student to leave as soon as he or she could throw each separate, uncrumpled piece into a box top placed on the floor three feet away. If I was really annoyed, I put the box in a draft.

Constant bickering resulted in a tour of the building. Each of the arguers was given an unsharpened pencil. The two had to cooperate to carry a ping pong ball through the halls using only the two pencils. If they dropped the ball, they had to start over again.[8]

School Discipline

> *I think it's like they're caught up so, the administration I'm talking about, they get so caught up in the job, and you know, like the politics of the job.*
>
> —Alissa

Sometimes your punishments are not effective, or school policy requires further action. The teacher's job is to produce a clearly stated office referral, which is

---

[8]This idea came from my father's stories of army life, where fighters had to wash windows, one on the outside and one on the inside, without smearing them. Thanks, Dad!

forwarded to an administrator for further action. Depending upon the infraction and the student's history, a discussion, corporal punishment, detention, suspension, expulsion, or even a criminal complaint may result.

Detention

Detention has been used since schools began. In the nineteenth century, detention supervision was not necessary. The schoolmaster would simply tie the miscreants to the desks and leave them for a period of time (Emblen, 1969). Today, detentions are often supervised by teachers on a rotating assignment, but probably provide more consistency when run by a regular aide (Chizak, 1984).

Superintendents and principals across the country agree that detention is an effective tool to reduce misbehaviors. As a teacher, I had both personal and professional concerns about assigning students who misbehave to detention. First, I lost control of the disciplinary procedure because I was required to assign detention based on a rule structure that was often incompatible with my students' learning styles and social and emotional needs. Second, the process contradicted my theoretical knowledge about punishment and its effects on behavior, a perception supported by the number of names that were repeated daily on the detention rosters. Finally, I had to supervise school detention two or three times a year, a duty I, like many of my colleagues, dreaded.

A Teacher's Reaction.   Detention supervision, a relatively brief time measured by the clock, can be preceded by days, or even weeks of dread for some of us. On the day itself, when the alarm goes off I awake with a sense of foreboding. What's wrong? Do I have a dental appointment? An exam I haven't studied for? No, worse! I have detention duty. Carefully I check my physical functions. Is that a tickle in my throat? A stomach ache? A sore toe? Can I legitimately call in sick?

In the morning I listen to the office announcements with growing unease. The list of students required to report to the office is endless. I hear the names of a dozen students, whom I know only by reputation, *bad* reputation. A few of my students are also called down, as usual, but I know they will dodge this detention rather than appear when I am supervising. I wouldn't know any of the thirty or forty students in the room.

After a day spent muttering about the inefficacy of detention, I enter the room on the bell, lock the door, so that latecomers have to go to the office, and call the roll. I identify the individual who answered to two names to help a friend and kicked her out. I quickly remove another student for talking. Having established that I am dominant and knowledgeable, we settle into another forty-five minutes of mutual misery. Most of the students are scared and penitent. They quickly open books and read or study. Another half dozen are scattered across the back of the room. We glare at each other. Eventually, they put their heads under their hoods and nap. I glance at papers. In about ten years, the bell rings and we all leave. What a miserable day . . .

National Practice.   Federal, state, and local legislation may regulate specific disciplinary practices. Students in special education, for example, may be punished only in specific circumstances.[9]

Large schools have a detention hall before, during, and after lunch. Detention assignments are the most commonly used discipline procedure to punish minor offenses. In 1919, students were punished by detention or another negative consequence for:

> whispering; note writing; unconscious vandalism; teasing; disobedience; truancy; obscenity; fighting; tattling; lying; stealing; cheating; gambling; showing off; bad odors; animals in the schoolroom; impudence and defiance; ridicule; profanity; hazing; aping college fraternities; use of tobacco, alcohol and drugs (including heroin and cocaine); vandalism; impudence; rudeness; and horseplay. (Moorehouse & Coffman in Weber, 1984, p. 21)

Today, detentions are often given for tardiness, disrupting the class, truancy and fighting, the use of profane language, failure to do homework, congregating in the halls, smoking, and impertinence. These behaviors are similar to those identified as possible predictors of school dropouts (Jozefowicz, Colarossi, Abreto, Eccles, & Barber, 2000).

Schools usually have a written discipline policy, given to entering students and teachers, and readily available to members of the community. The specific behaviors and their punishments are listed (including the size of a paddle and number of strikes per infraction in the many schools that continue to use corporal punishment). For example, a detention program in New York listed clear consequences for specific infractions: unexcused absence from class, abusive language, smoking, or gum chewing resulted in a one-day detention; the second unexcused absence or being tardy to three classes caused two detentions; and six tardies were punished by three detentions. Students had to report promptly at 2:30 and stay until 3:30; detention took precedence over extracurricular activities, teacher conferences, and employment obligations; a five-minute lateness resulted in an additional detention; students had to do schoolwork, which they had to provide; and a missed detention was cause for a parent conference and possible suspension (Chizak, 1984).

It is natural to detain students after class for a brief or lengthy conference about behavior (Pringle, 1931), but some detentions are meant to "annoy the annoyer," to

---

[9]IDEA, which guides current federal policy regarding students with special needs, states that students may be removed from class or school for brief periods, not to exceed ten consecutive days. If the removals become excessive, a behavioral intervention plan must be developed by the IEP team, which should include the student, a caregiver, a special educator, the general education teacher, an administrator, and any other appropriate support. This group must design and implement a plan to change the student's behavior through positive interventions (usually by finding and reinforcing a behavior that is incompatible with the undesirable behavior). If the student continues to be removed from school or the current placement, the plan must be revised. No change in placement can occur without a change in the IEP. No matter what the circumstances, a free and appropriate education must be provided for students with identified special needs.

mete out a crude justice by detaining students who are habitually late to class or regularly unprepared (Larson & Karpas, 1967). One of the major questions posed by proponents of detention is whether it should include counseling or schoolwork or force students to sit with their hands folded on the desk and stare into space. Is the purpose of detention to remediate behavior through advice and improved academics or to punish students with the exchange of free time for boredom, thus deterring future misbehavior? All agree that the rules must be consistent. Some researchers and practitioners claim that detention only annoys the student; it does not get to the root of the problem; and it is difficult to justly assign time in proportion to the gravity of the offense.

Research suggests that, for most students, a detention is enough to cause a change in behavior, but for some, it is clearly not a deterrent. Therefore, detentions should not be multiplied, that is, one detention can be assigned for one cut, but five cuts should be treated as a symptom of a more serious problem, which should be investigated carefully to enable a more effective response. Detention seems to be most effective when it is part of a clearly articulated discipline policy, when it is paired with counseling, and when parents reinforce the punishment at home. It is not effective when the cause of the problem is outside of the student's control (family problems, inappropriate curricula, teacher-student conflict, and the like).

Effects on the Student.   When a referral system is used, the student must deal with and please the administrator, who will assign the punishment. Later, the student returns to the class, either resentful of the teacher or victorious because the disciplinarian supported the student. Either way, the classroom problems have been exacerbated, not improved. Teachers should have the power to establish rules, clear consequences, and the amount of time to be spent in detention to avoid additional student-teacher conflict (Chizak, 1984).

Because the primary purpose of detention is to decrease unacceptable behaviors, research is often directed toward the evaluation of specific behavior reduction. No one seems to have questioned other effects detention might have on the student. Judith Herman's (1992) descriptions of the total control imposed on prisoners, hostages, some abuse victims, and other detainees sounds frighteningly similar to the controls imposed in student detention rooms. One survivor explained:

> We never thought of rules as fair or unfair, we just tried to follow them. There were so many of them it was hard keeping up. In retrospect I guess they were too strict, too nitpicking. Some of them were pretty bizarre. You could be punished for smirking, for disrespect, for the expression on your face. (Herman, 1992, p. 99)

Detention can be assigned for many misdemeanors, including gum chewing, insubordination, or oversleeping. It involves severe social controls and enforced immobility. Detention may have serious, unpredictable effects on a previously traumatized child.

A significant minority of abused children become aggressive themselves. One survivor ends a description of his incarceration for carrying a gun at age 14 with the following warning:

> Once a kid starts fighting back and becomes a delinquent, he reaches the point of no return. People should find out what the hell is going on in the family before the kid ruins his whole life. Investigate! Don't lock the kid up! (Herman, 1992, p. 113)

The Students Respond. In discussions about the purpose of detention, most students thought it was meant to punish slightly, to remind them not to break a rule again. When pressed, no student believed that detentions or suspensions were effective in causing behavior change, but in discussing specific instances, many admitted it influenced them to consider change. Some vehemently denied feeling punished by any school discipline. Angela maintained,

> All of the punishment that we've had, none of the kids respond to, I mean, not one of them do. And if they really wanted to stop, they'd stop on their own. This wouldn't make them stop.

Tom, who identified himself as a "late kind of person" said that the new tardy policy had been created because the administration was afraid that students would increase their lateness until they eventually ditched the whole period. He thought punishment was appropriate so that students would think twice before being tardy again. Tom believed punishment to be a necessary form of student control, because kids need to be afraid of their teachers to respect them.

Johnny suggested that the administrators have to eliminate ditching "cuz your parents are paying taxes, and then, they're paying money and then you just do nothing, not going to school to learn. That's why they get mad."

Tracy said teachers want to give the students a hard time, "Just to be doing it . . . They [the teachers] just like to kick it." She believed she was unjustly singled out because she was seen as a ringleader.

> He thinks if he kick me out, he'll stop my whole group that be talking. He thinks if he'll shut me up, that they'll stop talking too . . . But the people I be talking to are sophomores and seniors. I'm a freshman. They got their own mind. They older than me. They don't have to talk unless they want to. And they try to put that on me. I was like, "No, it's not my fault they want to talk. I can't . . . They got something to say, they're gonna say it regardless." It has nothing to do with me. If they would like to share their information, if they would like to share their business with me, then they can share.

Don saw detention as a sort of time-out and a chance to avoid suspension by figuring out behavioral alternatives. "They think you need time off from other students. You need to be in a quiet place, somewhere by yourself." His description of Saturday School was the most comfortable:

It's, Saturday School's like some come do work, but most people fall asleep, cuz you know, like, sitting in there so long, you be like, three hours, early in the morning, you fall asleep. But me, I just sit there, you know, just look at people; there ain't nothing to do in here, so . . . I guess that's mainly what Saturday School is all about. Sitting there and ain't doing nothing. Well, most people do stuff, but it's just, they just read, or some people play their Walkman, but I just sit there.

Rebecca said she had "no idea" why detentions were assigned at CHS because "You can't do anything in there." Later she talked about Saturday School and ABC as mild punishments and deterrents, but also commented that sometimes adults "want to do something, like if they're mad about something, they're mad about everything," and so they punish students. Sometimes, she added, their anger might be justified, such as when students constantly disrupted the class by coming in late.

Carla added that suspension also has a purpose:

> . . . Just keep those kids away from the school. Cuz they [adults] can't handle them, they can't do nothing about it, they just tell them to stay home. They don't know what to do. They don't, [they] just say, "Oh yeah, you're suspended for three, four days." And just call your parents to tell the parents, and that's it. That's all they do.

Angela also saw detention as a waste of time, coming from adults' desire to retaliate for rule breaking and to punish students:

> Yeah, take, I guess take the time away that, more time . . . Cuz you know, lunch is only thirty minutes and we weren't even out for thirty minutes, we were probably like out for twenty minutes. And then they keep you in detention for like three hours. That's way over how much the tardy took away from them or whatever, the way they want to think about it, I don't know. . . . I remember, when we got in trouble, and my friend, she, the weekend that they had first put our Saturday School, she was going off on a trip. And then the principal was telling her that she was just going to have detention that weekend, but he was just doing that to make her mad, I mean not to make her mad, but just to make her realize what she did was wrong and everything, and then later on he changed our date. So she could go on the trip. So he changed his rule. I guess they're just trying to waste people's time.

Alissa wondered what students were learning about living in the world:

> The guy that runs it, he was telling us that it's supposed to be a punishment and stuff, and he was like asking us, "Well, what are you in here for?" and some people said, "Cuz we got in trouble," and another person said, "Cuz we got caught." So it wasn't that he did something wrong, it was just that he got caught. So, I think that a lot of people's attitude is like, "Well, you know, I can do, if I can get away with it, then it's no big deal." And it's not that they feel bad about doing it, they feel bad about getting caught. If they had the chance to do it again, and they knew they wouldn't get caught, then they probably would.

Chaquan and Tracy talked about physical punishment in the local middle school. Tracy said her reaction would have been:

> Please, I'm gone. Be like, "See you!" That must hurt! Hold your hands up a long time. You put your hands up against the wall and you stand straight up. And you have to stand, and however long you have detention, however long you have to hold your hands up. You can't drop them.

Effects on Learning.   Unfortunately, managing the class with punishment had some real drawbacks. Of course, the kids were often unhappy, but that was a given in education. Learning, I knew, requires some boredom and suffering. But I found myself spending more and more time repeating the same things: behavioral injunctions, such as "Be quiet," "Sharpen your pencil before class," "Pay attention," and academic rules "Check your spelling," "Write neatly," "Use complete sentences." I made the same comments over and over. Would they never learn? How could I finish the text by June? I found myself mentally grouping students into the "good kids" who were learners, and the "bad kids" who were incapable, unmotivated, came from bad neighborhoods and so forth.

The worst kids to work with knew how to walk the line between annoyance and open defiance. They could identify my weak points and push me to the edge of fury by the end of the period, but they timed things so that the bell rang at the same time that my patience ran out. Eventually, I perfected the *look* and the *voice* and acquired the extra eyes and ears all teachers have. It became easier to contain the losers and teach to the kids who behaved properly and responded to my instruction.

Educators must also consider the validity of reducing the inappropriate behavior in conjunction with the negative side effects of punishment. We can infer from research on modeling that a teacher's punitive behavior will teach the student negative problem-solving techniques. We know that feelings generalize broadly, so a negative feeling resulting from a punishment in math class will feed a student's dislike of math in particular and school in general. Many students also resent the punishment of their peers, especially their friends. Students may also resist punishment in many ways, adding to the complications of administration and weakening the strength of the negative consequence.

Alissa expressed concern about the dehumanized assembly line nature of discipline in the school:

> I don't know. I don't understand it. I think it might be partly because there's so many students, and they really don't have enough time to listen to everyone. But, I don't know. I really don't know about that. I don't understand that. . . . I think because some of the people that, the students that weren't really concerned about going to class, they like to wander around, and be with their friends and stuff, I think that there's a way . . . I don't know.

> I think that they couldn't deal with those people individually, so they just made it like a group thing, to where it was, "Well, you know, I'm sorry if you weren't part of it in the first place, but now this is what's gonna happen to everybody, because of this group of people." I think they did it to cut down on the people in the halls, and you know, I guess they're saying, you know that there, it's less of a chance of a fight or somebody smoking or . . .

Many students in the higher academic tracks believe they are able to make their own behavioral decisions and resent the idea that they are being restricted and punished because less mature individuals in the school need stronger controls.

Since ancient times, educators have suggested that some punishment may be necessary, but it's not a good strategy to rely on. What is?

Positive Reinforcement

The specific attention to consequences, especially praise, has long been of interest to educators. Late sixteenth-century Jesuits used a system of rewards and punishment to encourage students to memorize materials; C. Dock, a Mennonite of the mid-eighteenth century, discussed the child's desire for praise and fear of blame as a means of establishing motivation; and the monitorial schools of the nineteenth century implemented the concept that discipline through reward and social punishment was more effective than corporal punishment. Modern behaviorists suggest the use of positive reinforcement to improve behavior. A positive reinforcement is any consequence that increases a behavior. Like punishment, positive reinforcers vary with the individual and the situation.[10]

Like punishment, the effective use of positive reinforcement requires some forethought. Once a reinforcement system is in place, however, it becomes habitual, and can be used naturally without the immediate negative results of a punitive response.

The first step is to identify the behavior you want to increase. This can be tricky, because school discipline plans tend to address behaviors to be decreased. The desired behavior needs to be stated in a way that is observable and measurable by more than one person. "Being good" is not an observable, measurable behavior because it is defined differently by different people. The behavior must be stated in positive terms. "Not talking" means that hitting, note writing, sleeping, and other negative behaviors may be reinforcible. Sometimes the positive behavior must be stated in terms more complex than the negative behavior. "The student will maintain acceptable behavior, as previously discussed and role played in the class" is a mouthful, but it does help you think about what you are actually looking for and construct a lesson or two to ensure that the students understand what you want. It

[10]B. F. Skinner's research provides a basis for modern educational applications of behavior modification. Paul Alberto and Ann Troutman (1999) have written a current, comprehensive text on the use of behavior analysis in educational settings. The Canters, James Dobson, and Fredric Jones are some designers of behavior management systems using behavioral theory (Wolfgang, 1995).

also provides a useful way for you to discuss behavior with other faculty members or parents and to set clear rules for the students. Sometimes it is important to note specific conditions in which the behavior will be reinforced. "The student will remain silent in class" discourages questioning and makes discussions or group work difficult. "The student will remain silent during tests and teacher lectures" provides more useful guidelines.

Establish a baseline by counting the behavior when it occurs. If it never happens, you probably need a smaller step. Baselines helped me identify and structure situations to encourage initial improvement. Occasionally, I could identify a cause for the behavior and change the environment, resulting in a faster change from the student.

Next you need a list of reinforcers, so that if students do not want one thing, they can work for another. Reinforcers do not need to cost anything or exceed what you would naturally offer to an excellent student, such as academic free time; restroom, water fountain, or library passes; homework exemptions; reading time; a positive parent contact; your praise[11] and attention. It is important to remember that the reinforcer must be attractive to the student as well as the teacher. The measure of success for a reinforcer is the amount the behavior increases.

One or two students in your class might need an explicit point system to regulate behavior. They might receive one point for five minutes on task and pay ten points for a trip to the restroom. Specific contracts, describing the behaviors, both academic and social, and the range of positive consequences, are useful in many cases. The discussion and thought entailed to design a contract can help the student and teacher clarify their needs and establish a basis for positive interaction. The paper itself can be a useful reference for all concerned parties. Remember, these points are not costing you anything—be generous! Once the behavior is understood and rewarded, the need for points or other immediate reinforcers decreases or disappears.

Setting achievable goals and making small failures part of the plan also ensure success. A student who misses three days a week is not going to have perfect attendance, and the first absence means complete failure. Instead, reinforce consecutive days of attendance, with the reward increasing as the number of consecutive days increases. Of course, you also have to provide an intrinsic reason to come to school so that outside reinforcement becomes unnecessary.

One plan we implemented with parents required a motorcycle parts catalogue. The student received points for each academic task he accomplished during the day—a math problem, a spelling sentence, a page read, and so on. That evening, he

---

[11]Besides being positive, effective praise needs to be specific: You used a wonderful metaphor in your third paragraph; You followed directions exactly when you set up that experiment. It is also useful to add an instructional challenge that directs the student to the next stage of development: You solved all of these problems accurately and efficiently—how would you handle these on the next page?; You did a good job using a biography to summarize Einstein's work—have you read any of his original explanations?

used his points to "buy" parts, which he put on a poster with his father. When Doug "built" a complete motorcycle, his parents purchased one for him then, instead of two months earlier as they had planned. We had to manipulate points a little, but the project was large enough and interesting enough that it took a full semester, and the motorcycle was purchased when he passed into the next grade. Doug also learned that he could succeed in school if he attended and did the work, providing a foundation to build on the following year.

Using positive reinforcement changed my class completely. The environment became friendlier. Good things had been happening all along, but I had discounted them as I focused on correcting my students' faults. And yes, behavior did improve, and learning did increase, as I became more and more comfortable with catching the good behaviors and responding to, rather than correcting, student work.

Being positive was tricky because I was raised and trained to find fault, but it wasn't difficult once I got the hang of it. Some simple changes I made were:

- I called or met with every parent at least twice a year with a report of student strengths and talents. I called the parents of the "worst" kids first and most often.
- Instead of marking answers wrong, I noted the correct responses. It was still (usually) easier to count the wrong answers, but I subtracted them from the possible grade to put the number correct on the paper.
- I rewrote the school's unsatisfactory progress reports to show positive behaviors and sent them home weekly. I warned parents to expect them; that no news was bad news.
- All students started with zero points and moved ahead during the marking period. All papers received at least a few points, which were added to the student's grade.

Identifying positive behaviors also forced me to articulate what I wanted, giving students something clear to work toward. They were able, sometimes for the first time in their school careers, to identify and follow a series of steps to success.

Once I began, it became easier and easier to find successes and pleasures in the classroom. Students began to value and seek positive comments and points. Grades consistently went from first quarter Fs and Ds to end of the year As and Bs.

Most critics of positive reinforcement do their research with college students or in neighborhoods where children come to school prepared for success. Some students do seem to need extrinsic motivation. Many of my students had never experienced behavioral or academic success. They expected to be bad and to be yelled at. They had to learn how to achieve in school and, more importantly, that achievement was a possibility. A concrete, positive reward system helped them figure out the school's systems.

It is also true, and important to note, that as they became involved in their learning, points became less and less important to them. Eventually, we just assumed an A grade and worked on learning and growing. That step was sometimes

Behavior Modification in the Classroom

1. Identify a specific behavior to change.

2. Establish a baseline by counting the number of occurrences.

3. Decide on a reward to increase behavior or a punishment to extinguish it.

4. Implement the consequence. If the identified behavior decreases, you are effectively punishing. If it increases, you are reinforcing it.

5. If the consequence is not affecting the behavior as desired, change the consequence.

6. When the behavior increases to 80%, reinforce a new, more complex behavior or fade the reinforcement gradually and sporadically. If you are punishing, continue to punish whenever the misbehavior occurs.

a hard one, though. Zach did a research project he really loved. He continued to revise his paper and add new data months after the rest of the class finished. He had to argue with his mother about doing work at home, because all she saw was that he was still working on the same thing. In school and in the drug rehab program, we were excited to see a delinquent grow into a scholar.

Controlling student behavior is a complex task, but without an organized classroom, effective teaching and learning does not occur. Punishment is necessary sometimes, but because of the time needed to use it effectively and the many undesirable side effects that can occur, it should be used as a last resort. Habitual, considered, positive reinforcement procedures are also effective, less time consuming, and often contribute to the learning process. Positive reinforcement is useful in working toward improved behavior, but does not necessarily lead to independent self-management.[12]

The Responsibility of Control

Teachers have a lot of power over their students. We need to carefully consider what we are doing as we help students establish effective behavior patterns. Are these behaviors useful in adult life or convenient to teachers in a traditional classroom? Do they interfere with other behaviors that may help students outside of school? How do they interface with the home and community cultures? When we react to

[12]See Lovitt's text (2000) for specific behavioral techniques to control behavior, improve academics, and encourage self-management in attendance, motivation, study habits, goal-setting, in-class behaviors, and self-esteem. Agran (1997) also discusses behavioral techniques to help train students with very low functioning in skills that lead to self-determination.

behaviors by punishing or rewarding them, what other effects are we having on the students? Will these effects enhance or weaken learning habits? How do they affect self-concept? What is the effect upon other students in the room? On ourselves? When is it appropriate to require students to change their behaviors and when do we need to look at our personal and institutional requirements?[13] How do we balance the needs of the student, the school, and society?

[13]Read back issues of *The School Law Bulletin* for interesting examples of questionable discipline practices: a student removed from a team because of a dragon tattoo (December, 2000); a teacher fired for giving students a choice of being punished by detention or electric shock (May, 2000).

3

Presenting the Curriculum

Cuz school is, come to study, come to learn, for your future.

—Nivek

Controlling student behavior is an important issue for teachers because student misbehavior interferes with the purpose of schooling. Teachers are not hired to discipline students, but to teach them. Depending upon your school, the content you are expected to teach is more or less prescribed by a state or district mandated curriculum. How does the content influence student behavior?

Many educational philosphers, including Kant and Locke, posit that deviance is generally logical, informed by a different set of circumstances than expected by the norm or dominant group. In New England, Harvard riots were ascribed to severe discipline and irrelevant learning; mandatory secondary schooling was difficult to establish because of the emphasis on Latin, rather than more current skills (Butts, 1947, 1955) so students were not so much deviating or rebelling from as reacting to inappropriate educational practices.

By the late nineteenth century, some educators believed behavior can be improved by adjusting the environment, so classroom structure and curriculum were recommended as means of controlling students (Crews & Counts, 1997). Others believed that clarifying the situation would help the student understand the need for compliance. It is clear that school practices can interfere with student learning, such as attention to completing, rather than teaching, a curriculum (Muir, 2000/2001).

Current management discussions include the concept that teachers should give students the same respect they expect to receive,[1] both in classroom interactions and in the choice and presentation of curriculum.

Like the majority of public school teachers in the United States, I am a middle class, White female. I enjoyed much of my high school experience and politely put up with the rest. I was in a highly homogenous academic program from eighth grade through graduation. Even though I began my teaching career in an upper middle class private school, the range of behaviors there dumbfounded me. Students who didn't like the lesson acted out, challenged my expertise (pretty easy to do at that time), and constantly questioned my authority. Their homework was poorly prepared, they did not study for tests, and often blatantly cheated. Oddly, they were not concerned that they did not meet my standards of behavior. I knew I was right, and they were wrong, but didn't have a clue about what to do, except to fall back on what I had occasionally seen in my school experience. So I yelled, called parents, sent students to the office, and plowed on through my lessons.

The Institution's Role in Misbehavior

The educational institution is often blamed for creating situations in which students are unable to behave. Although the student population has changed, schools have not. In 1900, 40 percent of the children eligible for eighth grade were enrolled in schools; only 10 percent of these students actually graduated (Doyle, 1978). Today, all students under the age of 14 are required to be educated, usually in the public schools. The secondary school population not only increased, but also came from different roots, with different goals and standards of behavior. Those who don't adapt to the expectations of the White, middle class teachers are often punished.

Collard (2001) reports that math students in a rural New England high school identified five desirable personality traits for teachers: caring, pedagogically skillful, just, interesting, and having high expectations. The students also identified six specific types of activity that helped them learn. They enjoyed field trips, clear connections to the real world, hands-on activities, group work, projects, and variety.

The CHS Students' Perceptions

As in other schools, general evaluations of the teachers at City High School ranged from horrific to wonderful. The special education students were at either extreme, with the general students being satisfied with most of their teachers and critical of

---

[1]Poplin and Weeres' 1992 study found that students and teachers may define "caring" differently. Teachers said they demonstrated their interest in their students by spending many hours after school in attending classes and workshops to broaden their understanding, preparing lessons, and correcting student work. Students defined caring teachers as those who expressed real interest in them as individuals.

some. Most teachers were evaluated positively, but the curricula and methods often received low evaluations.

The Teachers' Job

Angela said that the teachers at CHS teach well, but seem to be either too strict or too lenient. They need to control their classes, instead of stopping teaching because the students aren't listening. Don believed that good teachers would not have discipline problems because "if they're so good with kids, they shouldn't have no problem with their detention and giving them ABC."[2] Rebecca agreed that the teacher has to try keep the students quiet so that they can learn "the best they can."

When students discussed campuswide problems, they looked to the teachers for control, pointing out their failure to quiet one group and their success in breaking up another melee. Other adults, such as administrators and security staff, were mentioned only dismissively.

Both Tom and Casper admired teachers who acted firmly and promptly to remove a problem student. Tom said most of the teachers at CHS were "not that bad," but did not demand enough respect from the students.

> They have to act like some way that they're really taking care of their business. . . . Most teachers, kids don't respect them cuz they're not scared of the teacher. Some teachers are respectful (sic). You can just see it, when you go to that class. All of the . . . I mean, even if they're bad, they won't disrespect that teacher, if they know how . . . It depends on the teacher.

Casper remembered one teacher who didn't let anyone get away with anything. He implied that he wanted to be sent out of the classroom the first time he did something wrong. "Some teachers be like, 'All right, I'm going to give you a chance.' You know, see if you're gonna do it again. So, you keep on doing it again, you blow all your chances . . ." Alissa, too, wanted the teacher to maintain control:

> I think it's their responsibility, if they're [the students] disrupting the class, to let them know, "You're disrupting my class, I don't appreciate it." Sometimes you just have to tell a student, "You need to sit down and be quiet; if you have a problem with it, you know, we'll discuss it after class. Or if you really don't like it, you can leave and go to the office." Sometimes you have to say that. If they're like hyperactive, and they didn't have control over like, they had to take medication or something, they should, I don't know. Sometimes, I just think, sometimes you have to tell them, "Just sit down, shut up, if you don't like it, that's too bad, you just have to wait."
>
> The teacher draws the line. Because, you know, I can understand where the students need to interact with each other, and you know, feel like they're having more responsibility, but there's a certain point, you know, you're a child. You don't

---

[2]Academic Behavior Center, or in-school suspension.

know everything. You may feel like you do. You may feel like you're misunderstood or whatever, but for right now, there's someone older than you who has been through more than you have, and they're in control; this is not your class, this is their class, sit down and be quiet. That's basically it. Sometimes you've just got to tell them to sit down and be quiet.

But Alissa did prefer a friendly interaction with her teacher and her classmates:

> Well, that's the separation from, being in a training camp or like a strict academy or something. I think it's important to get to voice your opinion, and just share with other people, help you get to know them. Not really to be, not necessarily to be social, but, it's just important to . . . I think it might teach a little bit of consideration, to say, you know, well, wait a minute, this is what they're thinking. So, maybe I can do something to change, to make them feel more comfortable, . . .

Stephanie, who spoke highly of all of the teachers at CHS, became especially animated when she described an instructional assistant who is like a mother to her.

Interesting Teaching

Angela referred to the opportunity to socialize as being an important reason to come to school, but noticed that students rarely ditched interesting classes.

Carla complained about the repetition in math, but about not getting enough help in reading. Nivek had stopped studying because the teachers rarely taught, so he was confused. He said, "I'm not learning nothing!"

Rebecca pointed out that teachers who "explain things right" are interesting. She described a history teacher who discussed campus events with the students, listening respectfully to each student's version of the occurrence. "Each of us tells our own story and they seem to be different. So, that seems to be the problem, different people seeing different things, and that leads to problems." Rebecca also appreciated that they receive a lot of points in the history class.

Chaquan said, "I don't like this school, because the principals don't care." She felt that with the exception of a few classes, school was boring. The work was often too easy for her to bother doing. Chaquan did her work in biology, but not in Spanish.

> My biology teacher, she's good. She teaches us, she explains it, when she goes to the notes, she'll tell us how to do those, she shows movies and all that; I mean movies [about] insects and reptiles and all that. But my other teachers, I don't understand what they're saying. Like my Spanish teacher, I didn't even know what she was talking about. She would give us, like, nine assignments to do in one week. And then didn't explain how to do most of them. And she wanted to know why [we got] low grades in the class.

Some teachers are described as being boring. Rebecca said, that although they try hard, sometimes teachers are "out to lunch." In her English class:

> All we do is read and discuss things. Sometimes it's all right, if you read a story so you know what things they're talking about and you really get into it. But if you haven't read the story and they're talking about stuff that you don't know, then it's really boring. And for algebra, the teacher tries to explain all this stuff, and, like yesterday, my teacher was doing this problem, and she just started talking about it, how to do it, and all of a sudden she started going somewhere else, explaining something else . . . I got lost. So I started falling asleep, and I fell asleep. She was talking too much. Then by the time I woke up, I guess it was five minutes later, or ten, she was still talking about the same problem, she was still on the same problem. (*I am trying not to laugh*) So, but, I was laughing too . . . nobody did the homework last night. Everybody came today with the same question, "How do you do it?" Cuz nobody understood it and then she tried to explain it again today.

Neither Rebecca nor Chaquan worked when they were unsure of the material, but they were happy to participate in class when the teachers explained the work clearly. They both defined "interesting" as "understandable," and "boring" as "unclear." Johnny also listened to teachers who helped him, but didn't pay much attention to the others.

On-Task Behavior

Stephanie summarized, "A teacher's job is to concentrate on the kids. . . . Not them do her work or her do their work."

Casper, too, resented teachers who talked on the telephone instead of working with students; he enjoyed seeing popular movies and playing games such as Monopoly, but wondered how these activities contributed to his learning. He enjoyed having fun, but also wanted to work in school and at home:

> I remember one time . . . the teacher down there, he wouldn't give no one homework, cuz like no one ever did it. And I was like, "Can I have homework?" He's all, "No, I don't want to give out homework." I was like, "Well, can I take the math book home, for I can do some math." "No, I can't give out the math books. You won't bring it back." And so I never really had work. Sometimes I wouldn't want work and go home and I'd play and I'd be all, "Well, this is cool, no work." Sometimes, my mom would ask and I'd be all, "Well, he didn't give me any." . . . So no one would get homework, and everyone thought it was so cool and everything, but later on, even though I don't want to do it, if he gives it to you you're gonna have to do it and stuff. And if I don't get homework and everything, how am I supposed to learn and stuff? And Mr. Forrest, he seems like he knows how to teach a class and stuff. And giving us the work, and he lets you talk, but real quietly, if you get real loud, he'll just say that's enough.

A Good Teacher

Is interesting

Is relevant

Presents new material

Concentrates on learning

Several special education students complained that some teachers were not generally willing to help them. They proudly catalogued their accomplishments in classes where they received adequate assistance. Nivek said his algebra teacher explained things to other students, but not him. He felt that he needed more than two or three examples of how to do things and that class explanations were generally unclear. Although he believed that teachers need to know more about pedagogy, students, and subject matter, he concluded, "Actually, some teachers are all right."

Carla added that she rarely received new material, and when she did, it was in the form of a worksheet or page from a book, without supporting information. Casper and Carla frequently considered dropping out[3] because they weren't learning anything of value. Carla explained:

> And when I went to ninth grade, there was just nothing. It was just, I had to wake up early and go to school and not do nothing. I didn't have to even carry books, or pencils or paper, nothing. I never did carry nothing. And I don't know if it's just only the Special Ed, or other people, cuz I used to see, like some of my friends they would carry books, they would carry, you know, like, a folder and two books. And me, it was like, I never carried nothing. Like, you know, I don't know, I felt like I'm not going to learn nothing when I get out of high school.

Angela, a successful student, also complained of boredom, especially with teachers who worked directly from the text.

It sometimes seems as if students want teachers to be all things to all people at all times. How can we manage that?

Teacher Respect

Of course, teachers try to be respectful of others, especially of our students. But respectful behavior wasn't always easy to model. Sometimes—often—I had to be the initiator and model of respectful behavior for students who had not had much experience with it. At the end of a long week, it may be hard not to snap out at the

---

[3]Neither student returned to CHS the following September.

billionth rude reaction of the day. We all get tired and make mistakes because of that. As adults, it is our responsibility to follow up with an apology and an explanation of our reactions without accusing anyone. So, I might, as soon as I am again capable of civil behavior, say, "I'm sorry I lost my temper. I was very tired because I had a rough day." If the flare up was public, so was the apology. Students rarely felt they got away with something. Instead, they often returned the apology, and we were able to discuss ways we could interact more productively.

The students were also clear that teachers had to have control. In the beginning, this control is from strength. My students knew that I would punish and that the punishment might be unpredictable. Arm wrestling, horse talk, and above all Art's September visits[4] had given me a reputation of physical strength. Fifteen years of facing down obstreperous students in the room and in the hall had enforced their belief that I was "tough." That was my style, but down the hall, a tiny colleague who would clearly break at the first threat to her control handled her difficult students with a magic combination of authentic care and humor. Her students had more complex behavior problems than any in the school, but she had fewer discipline problems than any teacher I've ever known. Go figure.

Good Teaching

Curriculum is sometimes out of our control, but the delivery system is not. Students do want to learn. When they talk about having "fun" in school, they mention new material and challenge. What they do not want to do is waste their time.

Early in my career I learned the power of choice. We make a lot of decisions that can be turned over to the students without affecting the quality of instruction. For example, I might point out that we are coming to the end of a unit and due for a test; would the students prefer to have it on a Monday or a Friday? We have a movie about the unit; should we watch it before or after the test? Would the students prefer to go to the library or use the Internet first? We have to cover grammar, poetry, and expository writing; how shall we schedule the classes? Notice, I am still controlling the curriculum, but by giving students a voice in how we manage the class I increase interest and commitment. Somehow, they are more willing to do work they usually avoid when they decide when and how to do it.

It also helped to apply behavioral principles to my academic programming. Instead of giving points for behavior, I gave points for completed, accurate work. Instead of charging points for privileges, they were applied to grades. Students with a "C" or higher (as of the previous week) could have all normal privileges, including not doing the work. They quickly learned that misbehavior, or even just not doing the assigned work, resulted in a lower grade and loss of privileges. Of course, I had to clearly explain my requirements for each assignment so that I could assign points fairly. This process helped me keep up on my paperwork, documented student

---

[4]See Introduction, page vii.

Possible Grade Points

English
Free write	1 point/line
New vocabulary word	25
Worksheet	1 point/correct response
Reading	negotiated/page

Math
Computation problems	1 point/correct response
Practical problem	5 points/correct response
Conceptual problem	3 points/correct response
Explanation	25 points

Undergraduate Education Class
Article review	25 points
Chapter review	50 points
Book review	100 points
Teach the class	100 points
Classroom map	35 points
Lesson plan	20 points

progress, and generally clarified requirements for everyone, which improved the teaching of academic skills and objective information.

Student responses from both ends of the country identify similar successful learning experiences and expectations. Unfortunately, it seems that these well-known teaching methods are not used often enough to maintain the interest of many learners. Why? What happens to discipline standards when we change our approach to curriculum delivery?

Results

Positive reinforcement combined with interesting classes and respect for students should help you approach a consistently productive learning environment. If your reinforcers are strong enough, students should generally be task oriented. If your tasks meet student needs, you should be able to fade reinforcers quickly. Students who come to school with the occasional serious problem, which interferes with their ability to concentrate and may affect their behavior, can be treated with respect and given a day or two to organize their lives without affecting either their learning or the class room environment.

What Is Happening in Schools?

Basic and general level students find school and the academic experience stressful because they are constantly being evaluated in ways that preclude success. They must read inappropriate materials, write about meaningless topics, and solve mathematical problems that have no basis in their reality. They cope through substance use, outside diversions, and rebellious responses or disobedience to rules, becoming and remaining part of the discipline problem.

Climate is an important factor in school success, and discipline policies are important in creating climate.

> Highly punitive discipline policies, an overemphasis on control, and frequent adversarial relations between students and teachers create a climate that increases the alienation of students already distanced from school by their lack of academic success. (Wehlage, Smith, & Lipman, 1992, p. 32)

Educator violence, whether through verbal, physical, or emotional attacks, will erode, rather than enhance school safety and create a more violent school climate (Hyman & Snook, 2000). Sanctions on behavior seem to have little impact on students, but an orderly school environment may actually effect behavior (Pestello, 1989).

In a longitudinal study, researchers found that preschool and kindergarten teacher's evaluations of students as disturbing impatient, disrespectful, defiant, impulsive, and irritable identified children who later had problems with school and society as adolescents (Gottfredson, Gottfredson, & Hybl, 1993). Decisions about who will be a discipline problem are made at the beginning of children's educational programs. Traditional discipline procedures do not seem to have much effect on helping the children change.

Students do not see agreement or consistency within the school when specific infractions are punished: 62.5 percent of the students polled in one study felt that they were either not caught or that punishments varied unfairly. Of the students who were caught, 42.5 percent were merely lectured. Lower socioeconomic status students were sent to the office more frequently than upper or middle class students

(Lufler, 1979); students of higher socioeconomic status seemed to be able to avoid apprehension (Hollingsworth et al. 1984). In one middle school studied, 10 percent of the students received 45 percent of the referrals (Gottfredson et al., 1993).

As we learned from student evaluations of their experiences, some students, unaware of the rules or their consequences, feel their participation in the process is minimal. They believe that school rules are inherently unfair and inconsistently enforced. Some of the students, dissatisfied and cynical about the system, openly state their intention to continue breaking rules. Thus, the systematically uneven application of discipline codes may actually cause discipline problems.

Many students do not share their teachers' goals and values, so reject the curriculum as being irrelevant. Some of my most difficult students were very bright, but convinced they would die before they were 30. Several did. I lost a long argument with Billy about the value of an academic preparation for his professional goal—to be a beachcomber.

In our school, morning announcements included the same names for detention over and over. Stories were told of seniors who couldn't graduate because they had forty or fifty detentions to make up. Counselors claimed that special ed kids were a major source of trouble. Teachers complained about disruptive behaviors, but, I think, were more frustrated by their inability to reach certain individuals. I always had some students who were kicked out of one or more classes several times a day. They were unrepentant about their consistent infractions of school rules.

Cory got kicked out of class often and was removed permanently from several programs. He told me about one incident. A teacher of a required course individually quizzed each student at the beginning of the year so that the child could be properly placed in the program. Because he was in pullout programs and special schools to learn to read until sixth grade, Cory was unable to give information most children learn in elementary school. The teacher's response was, "What's the matter, are you stupid or something?" Cory answered, "No, I'm not stupid, and I'm not fat, and I'm not ugly, and I'm not old. You are." He took that course in the resource room.

Generally, loud, aggressive, disruptive students get detentions. In one junior high school, 6 percent of the students caused 57 percent of the discipline problems (Sabatino, Sabatino, & Mann, 1983). The research reviewed on the preceding pages indicates that students are disciplined because they do not adhere to school rules and customs, because they disrupt school procedures, or because they do not cooperate with school requirements. They are often students from cultures other than European American, with goals other than college preparation, or special education students who have been mainstreamed or included in general education classes without adequate preparation.

Repeat offenders are more likely to have a single parent, be of a low socioeconomic status, have experienced frequent moves, have had contact with juvenile court, have received lower grades, be less involved with school, and perceive schools as treating them unfairly (Lufler, 1978). In a California school district, the number of detentions served correlated with a grade average of C or lower, poor reading skills, poor health, and a minimum age of 16. In contrast to other studies, this district found no relationship to parents' occupation, number of parents or siblings at home, ethnicity, home language, or gender (Stanley, 1984).

Fine (1991) studied adolescents who dropped out of an urban school after repeated disciplinary actions. Psychological evaluations indicated that, contrary to common assumptions, students who dropped out were psychologically healthy and conformed to the mainstream U.S. ideal of nonconformity, especially by actively criticizing and challenging injustice. The remaining student population, on the other hand, seemed depressed, self-blaming, teacher dependent, conforming, and accepting.

Because many behaviors of minimally handicapped, mainstreamed students are identical to those for which detention is assigned, these students often appear on the detention roster. There is some legal question, and much public debate, about whether they should be punished for actions that seem to be a result of their handicapping condition. Detention, in-school suspension, and corporal punishment are included in the legal "lesser disciplinary measures" sanctioned by the courts for the handicapped. The teacher's duty to provide education for the entire class enables the assignment of punishment for such handicapped related behaviors as hyperactivity or impulsivity. The Department of Education Office for Civil Rights, however, says punishment should not occur if behavior is the result of a handicap. Current federal legislation (IDEA) requires a proactive approach in solving behavior problems.

What Is the Purpose of Discipline?

Instead of addressing the needs of the student, disciplinary practices are often designed to address the needs of society. For more than a century, crime in the streets was alleviated, in theory, by attempting to rehabilitate children in schools (Doyle, 1978). The public still assigns this responsibility to schools in many situations.

Because discipline is part of training students to become functional members of society, punitive procedures can also be used to winnow out those whose training would be irrelevant or inappropriate to the positions they are to assume (Fine, 1991). Greek philosophers explained that men are suited for specific tasks in society, such as workers, soldiers, or priests; since the role of education is to produce a governing citizenry, it is counterproductive to educate the workers. Calvin used strict discipline in schools to train and control citizens in his theocracy in Geneva (Eby, 1952).

Since the seventeenth century, when Harvard students were classified by social economic status, U.S. secondary schools' curricula, driven by college requirements, have treated students differently based on status.

Many modern secondary schools' vision statements spring from Bronson Alcott's nineteenth-century idea that instead of being controlled by adults, students should be trained in self-government, so that they could become responsible members of a democratic society. Civics classes and student senates work toward this goal, but schools still adhere to discipline and tracking policies that support a more rigid class structure.

According to the containment theory of behavior, it is society's duty to confine individual behavior to acceptable standards. Public education is a part of this process, but studies indicate that effective behavioral management through rules and reinforcement can only be clearly documented with White males (Thompson & Dodder, 1986).[1] Yet most teacher training and school discipline policies assume that it is the teacher's responsibility to control student behavior using variations of rule/consequence/reward procedures.

Most schools perceive the students as the source of the schools' problems; they do not consider the possibilities of inept administration, inappropriate classes, or irrelevant curricula. In 1903, Adele Shaw criticized the teachers, not the students, claiming that school routines caused crimes, rather than seeing schools as victims of delinquency (Doyle, 1978). Some theorists continue to maintain that discipline issues should be viewed as a symptom of problems, not the cause.

What Are the Social Results of Discipline?

When I look at schooling from a distance, I see students being taught to follow orders without question; indeed, what they see as common sense questions or observations must be ignored. Courteous behaviors, such as greeting a friend, can only occur between classes. Acts of support, such as listening to a friend's problems, explaining a confusing idea, or sharing knowledge, are all discouraged, sometimes with punishment. Authentic adolescent problems, such as bullying, sexuality, and the meaning of life, are ignored. Bringing them up may lead to arguments, noise, confusion, and other distractions, inappropriate for a contemplative environment. Students are taught to conform to a predesigned norm, which may be in conflict with their reality. They observe authority figures openly lying (We have no drug problems in our school.) and contradicting themselves (Academics are your most important responsibility. Football players will receive an extra ten points on the test because they had to practice late yesterday.). Commenting on these anomalies may lead to disciplinary action. Resisting them will lead to disciplinary action. Learning to live with them leads to—what?

Multiculturalists also question the need for assimilation, resulting in the loss of the home culture, in order to survive in public schools. When I reinforced certain behaviors and punished others, was I requiring my European American, working class students to give up other values? Did my African American, middle class students have to change their way of interacting to meet my needs? Are non-middle class, non-white students disproportionately represented in special education because of cultural differences? Well, yes, to all of the above.

It seems increasingly clear to me that current institutional practice and a large body of research are leading teachers and schools away from the goals of a demo-

---

[1]White females are influenced by these controls, Black males respond slightly less, but Black females do not appear to be influenced at all.

cratic educational program. But what can I do to change things? Maybe I'm wrong, and everything is just fine . . .

Some Activities to Try _____

During the first few classes of the semester, I try to create a sense of community and a safe place for disagreement, debate, and questioning. Many of my third- and fourth-year secondary education students are enmeshed in the importance of content and curriculum integrity. Others are committed to students' welfare without considering the academic functions of schools. Most are also very passive learners, looking to me for answers and absolute truths, which they plan to accept or discard after the final. Some also have very limited experiences with teaching techniques other than teacher-centered structures.

High school students seem even more concerned with learning in a safe environment. Most have learned about the dangers of asking abstract questions or making comments that challenge the text.

These activities gradually open a space for safe disagreement.

Introductions: Students are asked to introduce themselves by name and teaching goals. I go first, saying, "I'm Sue, and I want to teach preservice teachers how to work with a variety of students." As we go around the room, most identify themselves by name and subject area: "I'm Mary, and I want to teach history." This opens the floor for a discussion of teaching students versus teaching content. In math class, I might ask students to identify times when they use mathematical concepts, and I might begin by saying I avoid numbers whenever possible.

Opinion Walk: I do this at the end of class or before a break, so that students can be dismissed after the last choice. Students form a loose line across the room. Identify a center point. Indicate one side of the room and state an extreme viewpoint about education; indicate the opposite side of the room and state the opposite point of view. The students and I move to the site on the continuum that expresses our individual opinions on the issue. For example: Schools should be federally funded; schools should be locally funded; Schools should be federally controlled; schools should be locally controlled; High school students should be allowed to do as they please; high school students should be corporally punished or expelled for misdemeanors. After several examples, I ask the class for postions. This activity is easily adapted to most content areas.

Round Robin Discussions: These work well at the beginning of class, preceded by a quick write[2] to help students organize their thoughts. Quick write topics could be: Think about a time when you were punished. What was the most important thing you learned in school? How did a teacher help you? Students are then asked to briefly share their answers, and we discuss the responses in relation to theory and

---

[2]A quick write is a timed writing exercise in which spelling, grammar, and style are not evaluated. This is a good way to begin a longer paper or just to get thoughts, emotions, ideas, reactions, etc. out of one's head. They should not be graded, except as part of a participation grade.

current practice in their home and practicum schools. This activity is a nice way to help students focus on the topic for the day. It is important to allow them time to write and organize their thoughts before beginning the discussion.

Process Discussions: Modeled on one of the techniques used in *Voices from the Inside* (Poplin & Weeres, 1992), these are a way for all students to have an equal voice and to begin to practice listening to others. Students sit in a circle; the instructor observes and listens from the outside the circle. Students write down the three most important things they want to say about the topic. Choose a monitor, two timekeepers, two process reminders (to remind members of the group if they speak out of turn, argue, or other disrupt the process), and two notetakers. Going around the circle, each person either takes one minute to discuss something from the list, responds positively or adds to another statement, or passes. No negatives, questions, or debate in this session. Continue around the circle until everyone has passed. Besides encouraging quieter students to speak and more active students to listen carefully, this process is also useful in faculty discussions, at contentious PETs or IEP meetings, or in any situation where communication may be difficult.

Positive Reinforcement: At the beginning of the class, the instructor or TA counts a behavior such as elbow on desk or legs crossed and puts the number on the board. As the whole group discusses the chapter, the instructor or TA gives tokens or small candies to students who exhibit the behavior. After five minutes, the instructor counts and posts the number again. Repeat two or three times. Discuss what happens with the group.

Reinforcers: Try to identify 25 to 50 reinforcers readily available to the classroom teacher at no cost. Have your students do the same for themselves.

Teaching Opportunities: Students who want a more detailed overview of classroom management or whatever topic is under discussion could have the option of reviewing and teaching the class a technique to manage student behavior. They should come to the next class with a topic and a date to teach. (Presentations are not acceptable! Their grade is based on class members' engagement as well as learning.)

Content Focus: After talking with similar content area students about why they are teaching a specific subject, have each student write three life goals high school students should be able to achieve after completing the class. Under each goal, write three behavioral objectives using measurable skills. These will also be useful in designing IEPs with the special education program. Special education students at the high school level are responsible for bringing goals and objectives to their IEP meetings, but may need help in designing them. All students can benefit from designing their own goals because they begin to focus and identify personal reasons for learning a particular content area. Their responses also help teachers design effective curricula.

Behavior Focus: Some adolescents do not intuitively identify teachers' standards of acceptable, respectful behavior. After discussion in groups of several content areas, ask each student to individually identify behavior standards and write three to five rules that will inform others about how to behave.

Part III

Progress

progress

As the year passes, you may notice changes in your students and your program. Parents contact you about the program, grades, and other concerns. Behavior improves, management concerns shift from controlling students to meeting their academic needs as they develop their skills. You move through the text at a respectable rate, but something seems to be missing.

These changes may occur any time during the year, from the beginning to the end. Some classes begin the year with no behavior problems, and a strictly behavioral program may actually weaken the learning environment. Other groups develop during the year and outgrow the need for extrinsic reinforcement. Outside events may move the class in and out of behavioral patterns. In every class, there will be a few students who need a behavioral approach long after most students have moved toward intrinsic reinforcement; others who will be intrinsically reinforced long before the rest of the group. This means you are always juggling your management approaches as students react to the many influences in their lives.

Parents pay your salary, vote for your school board, and raise the youngsters in your class. They are integral to your relationships with your students, the habits and attitudes prevalent in the classroom, and the design and delivery of curriculum. It is important to establish positive contacts with them as soon as possible.

As young adults, students are learning about how to survive in the larger society. No matter what your content area, you are also teaching behavior. Students need to develop skills to observe, analyze, and reproduce behaviors to achieve their goals when you're not around to reinforce their appropriate actions.

More specifically, students are also learning information about your content area. Again, they need to develop independent learning skills in various disciplines so that they can continue to acquire and utilize information in an increasingly complex world.

The acquisition of self-discipline and lifelong learning skills should create the sorts of citizens that will succeed and contribute as adults.

The following sections will examine the importance of parents in adolescent lives, ways to effectively cede control to the students, and methods for student-centered learning in outcome-based curricular systems and large classes.

Will the results of these changes improve or damage the class environment and learning of students?

4

Family Influences

The parents' job is to help the kids learn more, too.

—Stephanie

The practice of universal schooling means that at an early age children leave home control for a large portion of the day. As the range of cultural, religious, economic, and educational backgrounds increase, so do different styles and standards of discipline. Educators cite poor parental support as a major problem in working with children. Discipline problems have been associated with lax supervision, inappropriate parental discipline, disunited family structures, weak parental temper control, poor marital communication, weak or no church membership, lack of parental influence on the child, and poor parental education. Block (1987) suggests that self-control, behavioral adaptability, and resilience, all necessary skills for public school success, are affected by the student's upbringing. Loeber and Stouthamer-Loeber (1998) point out the many correlations between parenting practices and aggressive behaviors.

Gootman (1998) found that in-school suspension recidivism is very high for students from dysfunctional families. Adolescents with parental supervision are less likely to have behavior problems, so school and family interaction can help prevent classroom misconduct and minor infractions (Deslandes & Rayer, 1997). Elkind (1984) suggests parents need to take a firm stance with their children, rather than giving in to teenagers who just don't listen. Doyle (1978) believes that teachers should begin their programs with punishment to counteract bad upbringing, then move toward self-discipline as quickly as possible.

The Students' Reactions

Once each individual student developed a personal sense of responsibility, parents were most influential in the CHS students' schooling. Rebecca explained:

> Well, they're the ones that are really supposed to be teaching us. They like, they said, people say that parents are our first teachers and always will be, so I guess they're supposed to help us through life, guide us through.

Angela's mother was angry because her daughter left campus, but explained why she was angry and why Angela needed to follow that particular rule. Angela said she won't leave campus again until she has a pass, partially because she prefers to follow the rules, partially to avoid Saturday School, "but mostly because of my mom, because I'm supposed to listen to her."

Johnny wouldn't mind being suspended and staying home to watch television, "but then your parents get mad." The students believed punishment from their parents was more effective than school consequences, but parental opinion was even more important to them. Other family members were also important as role models, supporters, and followers. School punishments sometimes affected student behavior, but, with few exceptions, students were influenced strongly by parent reactions to problems with the school. It was generally considered that deciding upon and administering punishment should be the parents' province, not the school's.

Each student had different ideas of specific things parents did to help in the acquisition of an education. Parents were responsible for clothing the student, getting him or her to school, and providing a place to do homework. They enforced certain hours so that homework would actually get done and provided assistance when necessary. Sometimes they needed to push the reluctant student to meet academic responsibilities. Parents also needed to be aware that education was not limited to the school campus and to teach their children life skills at home. Above all, they should encourage, support, and guide their children through school and life.

Parent Support

Alissa explained that her mother sometimes got angry with her and yelled, but she also made many sacrifices for her and gave her good advice to prepare her for adulthood:

> I think she's trying to make sure that I see I have to be responsible for myself; I can't expect other people to be understanding to my situations; and, you know, I just have to make sure I do things as correctly as possible. If other people are making up the rules, you do what you have to do to follow them. Until you're in a position to do differently.

Don felt that although enforcement of the school rules was up to the administration, parents should decide how serious the offense is in terms of the family's values and treat the student accordingly. His parents played a strong role in the formation of his values and the regulation of his ideal behavior. He spoke of them admiringly and strove to emulate them.

Supporting Parents

Rebecca preferred to tell her parents about a problem before the school contacted them about her behavior. She explained that her parents understood about the problems she had with school discipline because they had experienced them too. "But," she added, "if it becomes a very frequent thing, they start yelling at you, and then . . ." Rebecca wanted to do well in school, because she and her younger sister represented the family's last chance to improve through education. Thus, although school punishments were annoying, and made her "feel bad," she especially tried to improve her behavior to make her parents proud. "Every time I do something like that [receive detention], they lose more confidence." She knew that she should not miss first period, both for the content and the credit, but had a family responsibility that interfered with and superseded her need to arrive at school promptly.

Nivek, too, was aware of how his parents worked for his graduation and tried to behave, "Not for me. But for them, so they'll be proud of me."

Chaquan didn't like going to the office because the ensuing phone call bothered her mother. She was not punished, but her mother talked to her and advised her to try harder not to get in trouble. Her mother, too, understood the frustrations Chaquan experienced in school. Johnny's parents were easy-going, but he did not like to upset them, even when he knew he wouldn't be punished by them. When his mother got angry about the number of times he was suspended, he stopped doing things that would result in suspension.

Extended Families

Carla was angry at her parents, because they had not provided her with the home life and support she believed she needed to get a good start in school. They separated when she was young, and, in order to support herself and her two children, Carla's mother had to move frequently and work late. Later, after they reconciled, Carla observed both parents reading with her younger sister and encouraging her in school, but by that time Carla had already established poor academic skills and been placed in special education, where her education was hindered. Eventually, her mother tried to work with her, but they ended up fighting. Her parents are planning to reunite, but that would involve another move, and Carla says:

> I never liked it. And especially now, you know, I like it here and I want to finish school here. And like, we move again and I have to meet other friends, new teachers. And sometimes I'm scared, cuz I don't even know if they're gonna give me hard

work, or if they're gonna do the same thing they did when I got mad and I had to read in front of the class. I don't like that because I don't know how to read . . .

Her extended family also contributed to her mixed feelings about education. Most of her cousins were incarcerated or tied down by children of their own, but one graduated from high school and started college. Carla noticed her specific career plans, continued employment, and her constant hard work.

> And she told me, you know, "It's hard for me, studying, going to school at night, and stuff." . . . And we used to always get in fights, but you know, like now, we talk a lot. And when she was in junior high, she didn't know how to read, and I didn't know how to read either; I would just, you know, read little things, you know like little books. And I remember she used to cry, you know, because her mom used to get mad at her. She didn't know how to read. But now she's doing good. She wants to give me a job where she's working . . . she works and then she has another place; she works by herself and she has her own office.

Casper, too, was been raised by a single mother with the help of an extended family. He got angry when she was called into the office or court and had to miss work because of school issues. He would not start a fight, because his mother has told him to "just defend myself, but don't go up to someone and pick a fight." He told his mother when he ditched or got in trouble so that when his uncles, cousins, or sister talked about seeing him on the street, she would be prepared. His family encouraged him to do better than they did in school, so he said, "I could just drop out if I want to. But I want to graduate. Cuz in my family, not that many people did, so far."

Ana spoke somewhat wistfully of the days when she broke rules and had fun, but was firm in her belief that her responsibilities to her husband and son made it necessary for her to complete her education with no more disruptions.

Poor Parenting

Several students talked about *other* parents who "don't care." The students were pessimistic about the potential for friends from these families, believing that they were doomed to failure in school and life. Carla talked about her friend Mike, who dropped out.

> It's cuz like, I don't know, it seems like it's the way the parents are with you when you're little. They got raised with gangs, their parents were in gangs and drugs and all that. And they were never respectable to people . . . And at school, you know, they don't care. They'll talk back to whoever they want, whenever they want.
> (*If the school calls their parents . . .*) Their parents know nothing. They used to call his house every day after school. Cuz I used to live with him. And then, we used to get home, and you know he would leave the school and then he would come back and pick me up and (his mother) just used to just, "Oh yeah, OK, I'll talk to him, yeah, all right." And then his mom would tell him, "Yeah, what happened? What

happened at school?" "Oh, this and this and that happened." And she wouldn't say anything. She would just be like, "Oh. Well, go to school and learn something." And, "You're stupid." You know, it seemed like it was just a joke . . .

. . . Some people just drop out, and they never do nothing for their life, they think it's so easy, just dropping out. And they say, well, you know, "I'll have money later; watch, I'll get a job." And they can't and you know, they sell drugs and things like that and stuff.

Antashia, however, disagreed:

I've been knowing some of them since the fourth grade and up . . . It's like, they have those parents that don't care . . . You know, those families that, "Well, my brother's this" or "my brother's that, so I'm gonna be like this." You know, to me, you have to be yourself. If I was gonna say, "Well, my aunt is this, "or "my uncle is that" or "my mom is this." I don't want to be a medical assistant. I don't want to be a beautician and I don't want to be a policeman. You know, you can't follow anybody else's footsteps. You have to do what you want to do. Because when that person's done, you're following in their footsteps, you're not going to like it. Then what are you going to do?

. . . You can't blame nobody but yourself. I can't simply say it's my mom's fault that I'm here (in Saturday School). She didn't have anything to do with it. She's not the one I got in the car with. She wasn't the one, you know. She raised me, and she's not done raising me. But when I'm at school and she's at work, I know what I have to do, and I just chose to do the wrong thing that day. I can't blame her for it. You can't blame anybody really, for you getting in trouble.

Antashia also emphasized the role her mother played in helping her get her homework done and teaching her to respect the teacher, but reiterated, "The parents can only teach you so much. You know, while you're in the house. But then, as soon as you walk out of the house, it's gonna change, cuz you're not with your parent any more." Antashia also admitted that when she was discouraged or frustrated by school, it was her mother who pushed her on, by saying, "I want you to be the best. I don't want you to have to be like most of the other people today." She continued that she and her mother are equals in the family, both working to contribute to their economic survival.

A Teacher's Response

These comments are just about the opposite of what my students said in school. Although most respected and valued their parents, their daily comments indicated a desire for more independence and related attempts to establish personal rules and standards. Sometimes they seemed fearful of parents' reactions to their grades or behavior, but I didn't sense the respect the CHS students expressed.

Teachers and researchers often investigate and blame family life for poor academic achievement. Except for Carla, all of the students saw their own parents as positive influences in their lives, even though parents clearly interfered with some school expectations. We talk about communicating with parents, but do we? Or do we inform, instruct, and require them, just as we do their children?

Many urban parents do not interact with staff. Educators often perceive this behavior as a deficit, but there are often communication problems. Cultural differences create different patterns of interaction. Latinos/as discuss school with their children, while African American parents often volunteer in schools. For successful interaction, and to improve the school climate, parents need to be involved in problem solving, but as based upon *their* perceptions. Opportunities need to be created for parents to interact in a "supportive arena" (McKay & Stone, 2000). For example, Poplin and Weeres (1992) tell of an attempt to bring parents to a school to discuss their children's education. Invitations were sent out, refreshments prepared, but no one appeared. Experienced teachers and administrators shrugged their shoulders—their expectations had been met. Some researchers, however, rescheduled the event and sent out invitations in the primary language of the community. Most parents attended the second meeting and participated in a lively discussion.

Preservice teachers often ask me, "What do you do about parents who just don't care?" I don't know, I've never met any. I've met parents who are unable to care for their children due to substance abuse or other illness, unable to provide a good learning environment due to financial constraints, and many parents whose interpretation of the world and priorities for their children differ from mine, but I've never met parents who didn't care about their children. I try to remember that while I know about adolescents, parents know about individual offspring; I hold education, thought, and learning as priorities—some parents value training, skills, family, and religion more; I was raised in and have lived in a primarily middle class, professional world—some parents have lived different lives.

All of the parents I've met want their children to get ahead in the world. They can be an invaluable source of support in improving behavior and enhancing learning or they can sabotage the work schools are doing by their comments to children and their action on school board selection and district budget decisions. The students also claimed to value their parents' respect and sometimes monitored their school behavior in order to gain or maintain parent approval.

Parents with backgrounds like mine are easy to get along with as long as their children and I do not have any major disagreements. But, just as it is less easy to deal with students with different goals and values, dealing with their parents can also be difficult. The best solutions I came up with came when I treated parents as equals in our effort to socialize students.

The first step is to contact parents regularly, positively, and in different ways. Telephone calls, personal contacts, informative letters, student reports, newsletters, and school meetings are all useful ways to share information and ideas. E-mails, Web sites and listservs can solve the problems of conflicting schedules for parents with technological access.

A few telephone calls a week can usually (not always!) fit into a busy teacher's schedule. I did limit my contacts to school hours, but tried to make myself available to working parents during their lunch or coffee breaks. A telephone with an outside line in my room was a luxury that enabled me to keep really close contact with parents, but that only lasted a few years. Leaving a brief message on a parent's answering machine also worked. The purpose of these calls was to establish and maintain a good working relationship with the people at home, so they were always positive in nature. I tried to call the parents of students with the worst reputations during the first week or two of school. Finding a few minutes in those hectic days is difficult, but a teacher is rewarded by a good relationship with the family when the relationship with the student deteriorates. Additionally, I was forced to look for something good about a kid with "an attitude," and parent reactions of shocked pride, and sometimes cash or special privileges, caused the student to look at me differently, and tentatively try to maintain my respect.

Written contacts are also useful. They are more manageable in terms of time and individual attention, but they don't always make it home. After I computed grades, I sent weekly form letters to parents of students with a C or higher average, initialing three positive behaviors that contributed to the student's success. Some students delivered them with pride, some hoarded them to be used as needed or for personal reinforcement, and some students tossed them in the trash. Their reactions told me a lot about the value of grades and the relationship with family. Desktop publishing makes it relatively easy to create informative newsletters that can tell parents about what's going on in the school and the classroom. They should also include ways to contact the teacher and specific requests for assistance with re-sources, information, or teaching.

As students move toward self-discipline, they can take over writing letters of information to parents, telling about learning they value, work they have com-pleted, and goals they are setting. A teacher review for accuracy and a request for a parent signature can help some students design honest, effective communications.

Depending on the availability of technology in the homes, computers can enrich effective parent-teacher communication. Web sites, designed by the teacher and students, can replace newsletters with constantly updated information. Electronic mail enables private interaction without concern for conflicting sched-ules. A class listserv encouraging discussion among all of the members of the learning community is often enhanced by minimal teacher participation. Properly handled, such a list can provide valuable information, thoughtful contributions, and good modeling for using written discussions to understand and solve group problems.

When students are identified as needing special education, personal contacts are required by Individualized Education Plan procedures. In my school, the fifteen-to sixty-minute meetings were with the special educator, the parent, and other interested parties (students were welcome, but usually did not wish to attend). IEP design often turns into a catalog of student weaknesses in academic and social skills. Again, I tried to focus our meetings on discussions of strengths, progress, and next goals. With good behavioral data and documentation of academic learning, it is easy to have a meeting in which we discuss, nonjudgmentally, where the student began, where she is now, and where we think she should move next. Sometimes that discussion includes the fact that she was working three minutes each class and now averages ten minutes of on-task behavior. Few parents find lack of work acceptable; most are eager to help increase student focus and participate actively in discussions of how to do that.

It is easy to see how these techniques also work in the more uncomfortable meetings about a student's continued misbehavior. The discussion begins with a recognition of the student's strengths: He gets along well with his friends and has a great sense of humor. We move to the central concern of school—academic progress. He has completed 10 percent of his in-class work in the past few weeks. How can we improve this? After listening to parent ideas, the teacher can also bring up suggestions about limiting humor and social contacts when students are trying to make academic progress. The final plan should include teacher, parent, and student goals and identify the anticipated progress for the next period of time, ways to communicate progress, and consequences for student improvement. This procedure is currently required for students with officially identified behavior issues, but is useful for most behavior problems. It is sometimes helpful to remind parents, busy trying to meet their children's physical and financial needs, that their approval, pride, and attention are powerful student motivators.

The annual Back to School Night or Open House invites parents to attend and meet teachers, but interaction is often brief and one-sided. For a few years we had monthly class meetings in the evening. Both parents and students were welcome to attend and discuss current issues and questions about school activities. When I moved further away from the school, these meetings stopped, to the regret of many parents who enjoyed meeting others who shared their concerns. A beginning teacher I worked with designed a workable compromise that also solves problems with childcare and most work schedules. He reserves the cafeteria a month in advance and has students create invitations to their families for a potluck dinner. Students are given the option of family attendance or a home visit from the teacher. Most choose to encourage their families to come. Parents appreciate the opportunity to meet each other, see who is in the class, and socialize with the teacher in an informal situation. The teacher can observe complete families as they interact with each other and outsiders. With six classes, the teacher has to give up some free time in October, but the resulting interactions increase home support for the rest of the year.

Dealing with parents is an added responsibility for teachers with an already unmanageable workload. Is it worth it? To what extent does close parent-teacher interaction impede the development of young adults?

5

Setting Standards

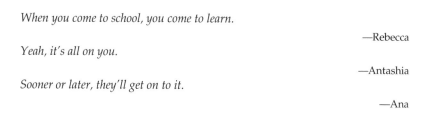

When you come to school, you come to learn.

—Rebecca

Yeah, it's all on you.

—Antashia

Sooner or later, they'll get on to it.

—Ana

Rousseau and other theorists maintain that behaviors are natural and developmental, so that educators can expect and teach around specific misbehaviors at specific age levels. The students also saw discipline issues as being related to their own developmental levels. They believed that, when ready, they would learn to discipline themselves.

Besides learning your content, the students are busy learning many life skills. Adolescence is a period of growth in "wisdom . . . knowledge about life's difficult problems" (Pasupathi, Staudinger, & Baltes, 2001, p. 352).

Adolescents must develop new and more mature relationships with their peers, achieve and accept socially responsible behavior, accept their physical appearance, accept a sex role, become emotionally and economically independent from their parents, prepare for marriage and family life, and acquire an ideology and value system (Havighurst in Klaczynski, 1990). These ". . . major life tasks are codetermined by the individual and the culture, . . . the effects of these tasks are mediated by the individual's activity" (Klaczynski, 1990, pp. 811–812). Specific actions, such as the orientation to social surroundings or long- and short-term goals and the means of achieving them, may be culturally defined. Since adolescents in the United States seem to value socializing in their early teens, then explore sexuality, and finally investigate employment as they approach adulthood, academics are generally a secondary or tertiary priority unless the student has higher academic goals (Klaczynski, 1990). Additional pressures may include conflicts among the home, school, and adolescent cultures and increasing independence from adult assistance and supervision.

Some high school students at risk for school failure have low self-concept, with a devalued sense of personal competence and poor confidence; an external locus of control,[1] believing that they have little control over their own lives, and having a marginal sense of their personal ability to effect change; and low academic motivation, often using informal, nontraditional learning styles. These students need opportunities for success, involvement, a sense of belonging in school, positive affective relationships with peers and adults, experiential understanding of the relationship between their behaviors and the outcomes, diverse learning experiences, and a generally positive learning environment (Nunn & Parish, 1992).

Rabbi Kushner sees teenagers as being angry, uncomfortable, self-conscious, and unsure. They are nervous and defensive as they try new experiences. "If we don't notice the tardiness," Kushner claims, "the disrespect, the disheveled code of dress, the T-shirts with vulgarities written on them, then they will do something more provocative until we finally notice" (Scherer, 1998, p. 22).

It is clear that the teacher has a crucial role in the reduction of agression and violence (Goldstein, Harootunian, & Conoley, 1994), but zero tolerance is ". . . a rigid policy which operates in a robotic fashion and does not involve any meaningful student discussion, but only succeeds in depersonalizing any respect for the student" (Long & Morse, 1996, p. 240).

One study followed best practice in containment theory and developed a schoolwide program that included clear rules, systematic rewards and punishments, home-based reinforcement, and a schoolwide positive reinforcement system. These changes did not significantly reduce problems, but when paired with reduced punitive measures and a school atmosphere of respect, support, and justice, behavior improved. Classroom changes also improved student behavior, although the relevant modifications could not be specifically identified (Gottfredson et al., 1993).

Gootman (1998) insists that misbehavior should not be tolerated, but also not necessarily punished. In-school suspension can be used for specific problem solving, counseling, and quiet work time. It will deter the student who occasionally misbehaves, but is not effective with students living with complex problems.

High school teachers and parents often wink at misbehavior because "boys will be boys," which may be why Fagan and Wilkinson (1998) found that girls have fewer aggressive behaviors than boys. Some adults believe that "raging hormones" cause lovesick inattention. Teachers try to survive, while teenagers grow up in their classrooms.

---

[1]*Locus of control* refers to an individual's belief about who or how life decisions are controlled. People who believe they are in control of their own destinies have an internal, or strong, locus of control; people who believe they are controlled by outside forces have an external, or weak, locus of control. An internal locus of control is associated with strong self-discipline, careful planning, and academic success in many studies.

Discipline can also be seen as an opportunity to teach students values about how to live together in a democracy. It helps them internalize community values, develop an internal locus of control; it helps students learn how to behave (Long & Morse, 1996).

Ivan Illich discusses the perception of childhood as a middle class construct, a product of industrialized societies. The youth of both peasants and nobles imitate adults to learn how to function in the world, but in industrialized nations, "work, leisure, politics, city living and even family life depend on schools for the habits and knowledge they presuppose" (in Rouner, 1993, p. 143). He sees this as another reason to discontinuing current, institutionalized practices, but Rouner disagrees. He suggests that, although virtue cannot be taught in schools, an appropriate environment will enable people to learn it for themselves, but ". . . we have to work at it. And school is the workplace" (p. 150).

The Students' Point of View

Angela, observing students who were constantly in trouble, insisted that they had to change themselves. "It seems like when you punish them more, they just keep on doing it anyway." Ana agreed in an optimistic vein, "And you know, sooner or later, they'll get on to it. They'll figure, you know, well, I have to do this. Stop doing this and do this."

Stephanie and Don believed that age is an important factor in deciding to change behavior patterns. For Don, ". . . all the principals, ABC, it doesn't help. It helped for me because I'm responsible, I know what I'm doing. They (students who misbehave) don't . . . I'm 18 and I know what I'm doing. They don't." He talked about how he didn't used to think about doing his best, but began going to art shows and thinking about art as a career.

> I be looking at stuff and just be thinking, man, I want to be good like that, to do stuff like that. So I thought about it to myself, and I'm gonna behave myself. If I could ace these classes, get out of school, go where I've gotta go, do what I've gotta do. No problem.

He wanted to get a good education and a good paying job to support his family. "I would like to be a better person in my life, make something of myself, educate myself with knowledge." He stopped ditching "because now I gotta get out of school. I gotta get credits." He believed it was important not to just pass, but to excel.

> I'm saying, you can't be a nurse, for example, unless you ace . . . these questions. So, you gotta know how to add, and all this stuff. You gotta know how to subtract, you gotta know all the body parts, and science. Ace science, then you'll be going somewhere.

Rebecca, too, realized that if she didn't work on academics during her last two years, she wouldn't get good grades and employers won't even look at her resume. "I'm trying to take more responsibility. And I'm trying to find a job." She added that she thought success in school is based on goals.

> If you feel like going (to school), if you think that that's right for you, then you'll go and look for help. If you just feel like, it's not safe for me, or I just want to live off my parents or just live off welfare, whatever, they're not gonna do nothing. So that's that. I want to graduate . . . (and then) make another goal. That's what a goal is.

The students were also aware of their immaturity. Angela said, "I don't know, maybe when I'm older, I can think about it, but now, . . . I don't know." Stephanie and Tom also referred to themselves as learners, in need of guidance from adults. Tracy believed that teachers and older students should adhere to a higher standard of behavior, due to their age and experience.

Alissa really wondered about how the administration arrived at the discipline procedures currently being followed. She understood that the goals were to deter tardiness, cutting, and misbehavior, but thinks the real purpose of school as a developmental experience may be obscured by these policies:

> It's not really, "OK, school is for the students, let's make sure they're getting what they need, let's get to know them, make sure they're getting along with each other," . . . because this is it. It's four years here and then you gotta go. Whether you're going on to higher education or if you have to get a job and go out and do whatever. I think they should be concentrating on preparing us, not what's going on all in the office, you know, on the computer screen. It shouldn't be, all about what's in the office. It should be what's going on in the student's life . . . I don't know if there's a word to convince that, but . . . I think that's what it is.

Self-Control

The concept of self-control, or self-discipline, is essential to many humanistic philosophies of behavior management. One must be able to deny oneself immediate pleasure in order to reach more abstract educational goals. In English schools, this value can be traced to Locke, who wrote, "The great Principle and Foundation of all Virtue and Worth is plac'd in this: That a Man is able to deny *himself* his own desires . . ." (Locke in Eby, 1952, p. 298).

Cognitive behavioral theorists posit that there is a cognitive, or intellectual, control of behavior, so individuals can be taught to understand the environment differently and change their behavior accordingly. They suggest that prosocial behaviors and self-control be taught through skillstreaming, anger control training, and moral education (Goldstein et al., 1994).

Some modern programs are designed to help students develop self-control so that they will comply with institutional standards of behavior. Being "held responsible" by an outside force should not be confused with being autonomously responsible. Students who feel they are being held responsible, controlled by an outside authority, do not feel challenged; they believe school is not a place for learning, and therefore do the minimum work necessary to satisfy outside authority (Bacon, 1993).

Self-regulated learning techniques lead to efficient, independent, motivated learners (Pares & Pares, 2001). Students who take responsibility for their actions, have a strong locus of control, and possess a clear work ethic experience few discipline problems, no matter what their family structure, culture, or socioeconomic status (Hanson & Ginsberg, 1988).

Teachers often believe it is their responsibility to control students. Indeed, the same students who sought independence from outside control assigned teachers the job of controlling other students so that learning could take place in the classroom. For themselves, however, students sought guidance in self-control rather then outside constraints on their behavior.

Student Responsibilities

When I spoke with the students, everyone agreed that their job in school was clear: It was to learn. Some were more sophisticated than others in explaining details, but all understood what they needed to do to succeed in school. Their descriptions of the components of learning commonly included listening to the teacher and asking questions to clarify instructions; doing assigned work when they understood it, including planning time to do homework; attending class regularly; and generally cooperating with the teacher. Students should not talk back to the teacher or disrupt the class. Above all, said Ana, a student should try; should do the best work possible. Nivek believed that good behavior was of paramount importance. He said, "People have to have the right mind twist, what to do instead of getting in trouble . . . or getting ABC or Saturday detention."

These ideal student behaviors were, of course, predicated on the idea that the teacher was doing a good job, which, as previously noted, was not always the case. Tracy pointed out that students should have the right to take their complaints to the administration if a teacher is consistently rude or unclear. Casper knew that the student's job was "to do good, don't give the teachers a hard time," but "anywhere I've gone, any school, I've given the teachers a hard time, most of the time." He said kids shouldn't miss school or be late, because they'd lose credits and might miss information or have less time to study. Unfortunately, "we didn't do nothing when I was there, but when I was gone or something, we did something."

Several students believed they had the right to break rules if they tried unsuccessfully to adapt to them. Antashia explained that her mother requested an off-campus lunch pass for her because she did not like the food that was available on campus. The pass was denied, because she was not a senior. She said:

> Forget it. I'm gonna eat either way it goes. That's me. I like to eat. I could eat some food, and I'm not gonna stop eating for nobody. You can punish me, they can have

me in Saturday School every Saturday, but if I'm hungry, I'm gonna leave and go get some food.

She reminded me that she was aware of which class she ditched and would only leave at lunch or during a minor class, but that other students "are gonna do what they wanna do anyway."

Carla pointed out that, although it was important to pay attention, one also had to avoid getting the reputation of being a "school girl." Casper added that students should not bring guns or drugs to school.

The Teacher's Responsibilities

Many educators believe that looking at students, motivation, or home situations as a source of school problems is a form of victim blaming that merely complicates issues. Instead, we need to look at what we can control: our own behavior in instructional and management practices and institutional habits that have become outdated.

If we demand that students follow rules of "civil" behavior that may make them vulnerable in unsupervised situations, but do not create a safe environment, we encourage them to "disregard and reject the school's behavioral norms" (Weiner, 1999, p. 68). Sometimes students do not trust the schools to protect them. Sometimes, obeying rules against fighting can be dangerous. Sometimes, the lesson structure does not encourage adherence to standards of behavior.

Carla's behavior was influenced by her teachers on occasion. She explained:

> Sometimes they get you in trouble, and like, they don't listen to me, and then that day when you come back, then you listen to them. You go, "Oh, shit, I don't want to get in trouble again, so I won't do that."

Besides affecting students during instructional interactions, teachers also influenced students' achievement in other areas. Don tells how he was positively influenced by two of his teachers:

> Teachers, yeah. Like Mr. Forrest and Miss Carson, they influenced me a lot, too. They say, "You got the talent, you can do what you want to do. But, you know, you gotta ace this class too, along with what you want to do. If you don't ace this class, you ain't gonna get nowhere you want to be, so, obviously, either way you go, you're gonna have to ace it or you just fail." So my choice is to ace it. So I ain't gonna fail. I ain't gonna be held back in school for the rest of my life, like most kids.

Several students believed that they need to be pushed. Again, Don used Mr. Forrest as an example:

> He'll push you, and make you understand, you know, like these are things you gotta do, then they'll work. They'll keep on pushing you and pushing you until you want

to go the right way. Like Mr. Forrest. Now that's a good teacher. You know, he'll look out for every student. Try to make sure you're doing the right thing. Keep you in line and all that kind of good stuff. Make sure you don't drop out.

Stephanie, too, appreciated Mr. Forrest's encouragement and confidence when she learned to drive in his class. Ana agreed that a push at the right time can help a student who is ready to change.

> Ms Guerrero . . . She's a good teacher. She helps you any way she can . . . She tries to push you, but not towards where you're gonna think, "She's annoying me" or "bothering me." She's not like that. She's like, if you want the help, you'll take it. If not, then just turn away the other way, don't take it. . . . She helps you. But she's like holding it for you, and if you're gonna take it, take it, and if not, well, just walk away and let the other person take it. . . . The teachers that we used to have. They pushed us and pushed us on doing things and stuff. They talk to you and they tell you, you know, it'll be too late, after you're gonna graduate, you know. You have to be a better person. . . . Well, you have to change personally first, you know, then to change everything later. You know. Cuz that's . . . some way, somehow, you'll end up.
>
> [If you listen to the teachers], you'll start getting on the right track, you know, you'll want to do more things, and then they'll want to help you more. More and more.

Many people say respect for teachers and other adults is disappearing. These students, however, usually demonstrated respect for their teachers in discussion, if not in behavior. Carla and Chaquan made excuses for the teachers who disciplined them inappropriately. Tracy, Johnny, and Casper were angry with specific teachers and criticized specific behaviors, but most students were reluctant to criticize their faculty.

Teacher respect for students is not often publicly addressed. The U.S. education system, designed by Puritans to fight the devil, rarely respects the learner. Curricula, standards of behavior and achievement, schedules, and associations are imposed upon students, sometimes in direct conflict with their needs and wants.

Looking at students with respect, forgetting my assumptions about teens and learning, was difficult in the middle of a crisis, but when I had time to think about issues and listen to my students, discipline problems disappeared. One example was our procedure for substitute teachers. During my first years of teaching, my absence resulted in student misbehavior, detentions, and even suspensions. Although I left individually designed work packets, crammed with assignments, students preferred to play. Experienced, qualified, familiar: No substitute was successful. It was easier to come in ailing and glare through bleary eyes than to deal with the wreckage when I returned from a sick day. Eventually, I looked at the students with respect instead of anger and blame. I thought about what it is like to deal with a stranger who doesn't know the rules, explains things incorrectly, can't find materials, and generally messes up. Life is hard enough. I'd have some fun while I could. So, because working with a stranger can be more difficult than usual, I offered students double points for all of the work completed with a substitute teacher. The sub was asked to remind the students of the new policy each period and to sign each work sheet as it was turned in. Behavior changed dramatically. As long as I left enough work, students were too busy to act up. Yes, there were still occasional problems, such as students doing a lot of homework to pass in if I was out for several days and increased concern for/fostering of my weak health toward the end of the marking period, but we worked things out. Teacher respect for students can avert many discipline problems. When we think the best of our students and look for ways to meet their learning needs, they may not need to rebel or resist.

Teachers have to look at students through many different lenses. We have to be good psychologists, understanding the students' perceptions. We have to know what to say and when to say it. We have to know when and how to push, and when it is better to back off. We have to have faith in our students, even though sometimes the students do not seem ready or able to succeed. We also need to provide academic information and raise our personal standards as well as our expectations for students.

Culture and Race

Schooling usually emphasizes basic values, norms, and social skills appropriate to European American bureaucratic settings. But the United States is a nation that is especially rich in diversity, and our children from different backgrounds bring different values, behaviors, motivations, and goals to schools. Among certain ethnic minorities, a relative lack of learning in formal classroom situations and problems with school functioning have been evident for more than a century (DeVos & Suárez-Orozco, 1990). Values, beliefs, and attitudes about education are sociocultural elements that include the assumed goals of schooling, appropriate means of achieving them, and the roles and responsibilities of teachers, children, and parents. Understanding the variations in these makes a difference in dealing with students from other cultures, who may read different meanings into physical distance, eye contact, closed posture, and teacher/student responsibilities (Kleifgen, 1988). "Generally, dominant group members, such as white Americans, ascribe to themselves the proper moral values, cultural norms, good manners, good and correct speech, and good and correct posture" (Haynes in Ogbu, 1987, p. 320). Truancy and absenteeism have been especially high among recent immigrants and among African Americans since before the turn of the century (Doyle, 1978). Thus, conflict occurs when the student places family and friends above school attendance rules or chooses to read the sports pages instead of the prescribed English literature selections.

The differences in values and habits of interaction between the original population of the United States and the current dominant group results in many misunderstandings in schools. For example, the European American culture assumes that it is the right and responsibility of adults to control their youth. Native Americans, on the other hand, generally teach behavior by example and subtle hints (Cleary &

Peacock, 1998). Deyhle and LeCompte (1994) chronicled the cultural mismatch of Anglo teachers and administrators with Navajo students and their families. The educators designed a new middle school using the most current theories of child development and best practice for educating 11- to 15-year-olds. Conflicting priorities, opposing theories of adult responsibilities, contradictory child-rearing practices, and different value systems combined to create misunderstandings between school and community. Culturally appropriate behaviors, which conflicted with well-intentioned rules and policies rooted in another culture, led to discipline problems in the school.

Recent, voluntary immigrants may see school learning as a way to add to current skills (Gibson, 1987), but they often need school support to demystify differences and learn to conform to the different expectations and values of a new culture (Delgado-Gaitan, 1988). Involuntary minorities may equate these adaptations with a loss of ethnic culture and resist them. Both groups realize that cultural conformity is the price most schools set for success, which may be seen as a diploma, not necessarily an education (Delgado-Gaitan, 1988; Gibson, 1987). Although some clearly understand the importance of formal education in the battle against oppression and the struggle to achieve goals, the price—a loss of culture and language—is often too high to pay. Some Alaskan Native Americans associate the acquisition of literacy skills with the betrayal of their own ethnic identity and refuse to learn in school as a means of resistance (Erickson, 1987).

As minority students' cultural understandings come into conflict with teachers', both build reputations and relationships that spiral into frequent disciplinary actions. For example, the misuse or alternative use of language leads to discriminatory discipline practices in schools (Collins, 1988). Subtle differences in speech patterns, narrative styles, and social interactions are a source of frustration to both student and teacher (Erickson, 1987; Fordham, 1993). Hall (1966, 1983) discusses variant preconscious perceptions of time and space that cause frequent individual and institutional conflicts in multicultural interactions.

Misalignment of cultural values and assumptions often leads to misunderstandings. As the percentage of minority students in a school increases, attendance decreases (Ray, 1991), perhaps because of the level of discomfort the students may experience within the school culture.

Additionally, the content and information presented through the canon often marginalizes, silences, misinterprets, and misinforms (Blair, 1994). Students from non-White, non-middle class backgrounds often have a difficult time seeing themselves presented with any accuracy, and many react in a negative manner.

In some communities, students are members of a national minority, but are a numerical majority within the school. Because most teachers are of the national majority culture, the institutional culture clearly reflects that of the nationally dominant group (Patthey-Chavez, 1993).[2] Additionally, most public school texts are

---

[2]"Dominant" does not refer to the majority, but rather the controlling group. Membership is often limited not only by race and gender, but also by class, religion, ethnicity, and neighborhood.

published by the dominant group, education law is enacted by a dominant legislature, media resources are controlled by members of the dominant group, and so on. It seems impossible to escape the dominant cultural viewpoint, especially when teachers and administrators have been educated in the same system and share the assumptions of the dominant group.

Culture and Race to a White Teacher

When I was teaching, negative assumptions about people were strongly deplored and firmly ignored. They were bad, they were there, live with it. So here I need to apologize to all of my students for the injuries I did by ignoring their race, religion, sexuality, class, and appearance.

Taisha, I still cannot forget the day you came to me after lunch, asking why White students were making such cruel comments about your race. "Ignore it," I said. "They're stupid. They're wrong. You have to move beyond it." I didn't know what else to say. Your pain made me uncomfortable, so I chose to brush it aside. I hope you met up with a more courageous person eventually and explored racism in more depth. Knowing you, you found a way to begin to answer your question. I'm sorry I didn't take the opportunity to learn with you. I'm *deeply* sorry I trivialized an important question.[3]

Facing up to Taisha's question would have opened wounds and caused painful, heated arguments, unacceptable in our high school culture. I'll bet it also would have averted some other discipline problems and led to real learning for all of us.

Addressing real-life problems is part of the learning that happens in schools. Students I know, including those who share their ideas here, are learning to ignore problems, to get around rules, and to solve differences through displays of strength and power. I learned the same lessons in my school days, but am increasingly unhappy with the way they have affected my life.

Decision Making

Current schooling methodologies are incompatible with some cultures, and testing and labeling consistently underestimate abilities.[4] Because no one teacher or administrator can understand all of the different cultures present in schools in the United States, educators need to be aware of the many possibilities of acceptable behaviors and communications, in a culture-general sense, so that they can expand their personal bases of multicultural understanding and classroom interactions (Varney

---

[3]Other White teachers beginning to deal with racism in the school might find Beverly Tatum's (1997) work useful.

[4]For example, Vélez-Ibáñez and Greenburg (1992) discuss Latino-Anglo interactions in a Los Angeles high school.

& Cushner, 1990).[5] It is also important to remember because behavior is affected by many factors, and students adapt selectively from the choices presented to them, so educators cannot assume that all children in one culture will have the same values, motivations, goals, and beliefs. Each student must always be observed and treated individually to allow for variations in behavior (Weisner, Gallimore, & Jordan, 1988).

Weiner (1999) compares understanding the possibilities of various cultures to a doctor's knowledge of chest pain: The doctor must still diagnose the pain as indigestion or heart attack and treat it accordingly; the teacher must still evaluate and react to behavior in specific situations with specific individuals. A White teacher was angry about teaching multinational immigrant children because she didn't understand their responses and needs. She blamed her lack of training until she realized "my students were my resources all along. They come equipped with all the tools" (in Weiner, 1999, p. 59). Although they still had the challenge of learning a new language, her students were able to explain their culture and did have the cognitive abilities necessary to develop academic skills. Weiner explains, "I think that the most successful urban teachers regard their students as people from whom they have much to learn as well as teach. They and their students regard the community as a classroom, as a community or family in which everyone's talents and abilities are respected" (p. 59). I can attest to the value of this philosophy in rural schools, too!

Motivational and disciplinary techniques have been successfully adapted and applied to children who seem to have a culturally based conflict with public schools. Although cultural conflicts may be very narrow and are often specific to one culture, they still present subtleties that are critical for school success. The identification and implementation of culturally compatible teaching styles (such as indirect praise of a group or specific praise of an individual, scolding individuals or groups, immediate or delayed action) resulted in improved behavior and increased learning in Hawaiian and Navajo classes (Vogt, Jordan, & Tharp, 1987). In a preponderantly Mexican American school, student success was increased and behavior problems decreased by working on self-image, visions for the future, and community action instead of focusing on an individualistic goal of college preparation (Abi-Nader, 1990). "Culturally responsive pedagogy . . . can reduce miscommunication by teachers and students, foster trust, and prevent the genesis of conflict . . ." (Erickson, 1987, p. 355).

The students I talked with referred to some of the conflicts identified by researchers, but did not identify them as cultural or as being the result of dominance by one group. It was clear, however, that cultural and racial conflicts existed in the school. Some came from the outside, but they were also tightly woven into the

---

[5]Edward T. Hall (1966, 1983) writes about subtle variations in daily behavior that can cause conflict with academic expectations. Sonia Nieto (1996) and Christine Sleeter address schools more directly. Peace Corps publications, urban school districts, and specific religious organizations can also provide information about cultural differences that can lead to misunderstandings in the schools. *Anthropology and Education Quarterly* and *Multicultural Education* are two journals that address school and community culture.

curricula, institutionalized procedures, and assumptions of schools. They affected the learning community in many ways. Because of the riots, our conversations at CHS also included some discussion of racism and race relations in the community.

Race

I don't know about that. I don't know.

—Johnny

All of the students appeared to be in the process of developing their ideas about race. Some were positive about the race relations on campus; most were unsure. They did not perceive teachers as being racially motivated. A few made comments that indicated a conflict between what they thought was acceptable to say to me as a European American and what they really felt.

Chaquan told me of one substitute who was no longer hired because of calling a girl a racially pejorative name. Nivek believed that some teachers are all right, but others:

> have this racial way too. Bad manners. Because some teachers have their own historical problems, and I don't like to hear that stuff around me, because I just feel, people who hate each other, I don't like that. So like, people, the teachers, that, they like, Black teachers, have their own thing, only for Black history and everything like that. You see those different histories, and they just talk about only their own, Black people and like that. Instead of different . . . I'm not particularly happy about it. They just talking about one thing, instead of all the peoples here. We're all human, you know. We all have to take care of each other, too. To take care of each other, because, whatever happens around the world, you will not see anybody in, you know, you and I hang around with anybody, be together.

Antashia saw racial conflict as being illogical. "Mexican and Black. It's like we're all practically the same color. It's stupid. We all, you know, instead of one group trying to have power over the other group, we should all come together. It's stupid . . ." Nivek, who said all his friends are different, was more emotional. "The racial stuff? It's not right to be in the school. It's not good to be around the school. It's like hating each other every day. Having so much problems in school. It's not very good."

Don said some of his friends will say they hate Mexicans, and he has heard acquaintances say they hate Blacks, but, "They're cool, you know. If you don't have a problem with the Mexicans, they won't have a problem with you, see. . . . The point is, all the Black kids gotta look at it." He went on to explain that Blacks have a language style that includes "messing with" that may be misunderstood by second language learners.[6] He concluded, "Well, you know, you gotta understand each other, you gotta talk a way that everybody understands."

---

[6]See Kochman (1983), *Black and White Styles in Conflict,* for more information on communication differences.

Many students talk about friends from other races. Ana insisted, "I have friends that are White, I have friends that are Black, and Chinese, Samoan, everything." Antashia chose her friends based on their behavior.

> [I choose my friends] in my classes. You know, you *know* them. Like, to me, it's like, don't be . . . my friend and then as soon as we walk out of class, you looking at me stupid. You know, if you're gonna speak to me, speak to me. I don't have a problem with that. I don't have any problem with anybody. You know, a person is a person. So it doesn't matter what color they are, or how you made your friend . . .

Alissa, too, chose her friends based on traits other than race:

> I have lots of different friends. I have racially mixed friends, I have a Hawaiian friend. I personally, I don't really look at your color for you to be my friend. Whether you kind of accept me and let me be who I am, are we comfortable around each other, do we have things in common? I don't really look for, "Oh I want this big group of Black friends," or, "Oh, I don't like Black, I only want this big group of Latino friends, because of how Blacks are." I don't do it like that. I go by how they treat me, and, you know, if I see, like somebody needs help, or . . . we're going to the same activity, it's like, well, you know, let me try to get to know them so I'll feel, we'll feel a little bit more comfortable, that's how I go about friendship. I don't go by color.

But she recognized the existence of racial conflict within the school:

> There's definitely a lot of stress between the races. It's like, like a control/power kind of thing, where you know, feel like I'm being, um, I don't know how to say it. Not like endangered, but I feel like there's more of you, so I have to stay tough and be strong, and make sure, you know, you don't cross whatever line I think should be. Um, it definitely got out of hand.

Other students also referred to feeling uncomfortable, or even endangered at times, especially during the days after the riots. Chaquan explained that she refused to return to her class after the first riot because there were a lot of Mexicans in it. Carla reluctantly admitted that she felt uncomfortable at CHS because there were more Blacks than Mexicans in the school. ". . . When there's a lot of Mexicans at a school, and there's just a little bit of Blacks, the Mexicans take control. And when there's a lot of Blacks, and not many Mexicans, they want to take control of the school." Johnny explained that he and his family were willing to socialize with Blacks, but his sister would not be permitted to marry an African American. When he fights an African American, he checks the ratio of Latinos and Blacks around him.

Several comments also indicated a kind of score-keeping attitude between the African Americans and Latinos. Antashia believed that the music broadcast over the public address system at lunch time should be discontinued because it causes so many arguments—each group believes the other's style is favored. Rebecca talked about the tensions on Columbus Day, when Latinos wanted to leave school to picket City Hall and the Black students did not support them. Latinos complain about a month dedicated to African American studies, while Blacks counter with the day-long party to celebrate Mexican Independence Day. Both groups talk about the other's getting away with breaking school rules with impunity.

Alissa was the only student to speak of personal experiences with racial prejudice, and her conflicts were with her own group:

> There's only a small handful of people that I call friends. Most of them are not Black. That's the truth. Most of them aren't. Because I find, that I'm considered, you know, in my community, I'm considered fair-skinned. Black people have stereotypes about other Black people . . . I don't know if they feel threatened, or they just feel the need to trip. But they don't always accept you, or get to know you before they make judgments. They'll just make the judgments and say, "Well, that's how I feel." I find that, to me, other cultures, they're more willing to get to know you first. I don't know if it's the individuals. It might be, I could say, it's just the individual person, and they were willing to get to know me. But, if I was going by groups of people, I haven't been real accepted by [the Black students]. I've been told for lots of different reasons. You know, because I choose to read this, you know, or my English, because I don't use a lot of slang all the time, or how I dress, or whatever the reason is. I haven't always been accepted, in [Black groups] . . . I don't know.

One of the real-life problems we see in school is the conflicts of diverse cultures in a monocultural institution. Institutional procedures, designed for middle and upper class heterosexual Anglo males, do not reflect the learning needs of most modern students. After three centuries, it may be time to make some changes in the curriculum. It was relatively easy for me to actively work on curricular enrichment that included middle class heterosexual Anglo females, but then things started to get fuzzy. As I explore various histories, traditions, means of communication, behaviors, and so on, it's just gotten more confusing, but my life has been enriched immeasurably. Isn't that what education is all about?

What changes can be made by the school itself? Should changes be made? If you believe that students should be assimilated into the dominant culture, the answer is clearly, "No institutional changes are neccessary." If you believe that schools should reflect and adapt to the students' home cultures, then the institutions have to change radically; each school will have a unique style and teach a different set of rules, facts, skills, and concepts. Schools that do not have a clear cultural majority or schools in communities that are experiencing cultural changes would have to constantly adapt. Seems like the first point of view is much easier to maintain, while the second is more respectful of the diverse needs of our learners. Is there a third option? What *should* schools look like?

6

Adjusting the Curriculum to Student Needs

As we ask students to assume more responsiblity in their learning, several problems arise, all rooted in the concern that they'll not be able to handle curricular decisions. We fear that students will want to play rather than work; we suspect that cultural values will deviate from standard curricula; we know that we do not know about much of the material students will want to study. Above all, responsible teachers worry that in creating a student-centered program, we will fail in our responsibility to prepare them to be successful in the adult world.

Playing Games

Sometimes they do the opposite of the rule. Just to do it.

—Tom

Sometimes, people have conflicting goals. The students contradicted themselves when they talked about their responsibilities to learn and their need to socialize. Occasionally teachers or administrators may declare a work-free day or present a really fun activity (in the student's opinion as well as the teacher's). Whether they feel like working or not, the students have a day off. But adults rarely design enough amusement into a program to meet an adolescent's need for fun, and what they do allow includes only a fraction of student ideas and opportunities. Breaking the rules and getting away with it can be a fun activity.

Playful behavior among adolescents at work and in school includes horseplay, pranks, joking, and other forms of humor. Males make fun of females. Humor is used to test boundaries of social relations, create solidarity among members of groups, and enforce status patterns (Borman, 1988). Salend and Salend (1986) contend that teachers do not value humor highly. Conflicts in behavior and attitude between teachers and adolescents may well contribute to discipline problems.

As we conversed, it became clear that students knew the rules fairly well and generally broke rules because they had other priorities. Some students were needed at home, others depended on another person to get to school on time; some were bored with school or had someplace else to go; a few were defending their person or their honor, a few were falsely accused. Some situations, however, seemed inexplicable, until we started talking about game playing, when all of the students agreed that there was an element of sport in school discipline. The game seems to have at least two variations: teasing teachers and proctors is one goal; getting around the rules is another.

The students all denied any feeling of malice or anger when playing with the system. Antashia referred to the game as a joke. Ana said, "It's fun, because, you know, you can't be boring all your life. You know, you have to get some excitement in your life. So . . ." She believed that without rules, school would be boring. Her husband explained, "It's more like a gamble; it's like, if you can get away with it, you don't get in trouble. But if you get caught, you're in trouble. You're taking a chance. The excitement of trying to get away with it." Carla clarified, "Sometimes you get lucky and sometimes you don't."

Controlling Time

Robert told one of his favorite ways to beat the system:

> Don't go to things, like you're gonna skip a class, you go to a class your friend's in, or you go to a class where there's a substitute, a substitute teacher.
>
> I'd go to, there'd be a substitute in like, an art class, I'd ditch PE, just to go to Art. I didn't even have Art. I'd go and sit in there, you know, and talk to my friends and stuff during that period and then if I had other friends in the next period, I'd do the same thing . . .

Or, he suggested, "Like the teachers, you make them think that they needed something. 'Oh, you're out of this! I'll go get some.'" Ana added, "Or like you use the excuse that you need to go to the bathroom . . . and you're out, and your friends also make passes for you . . ." Robert continued:

> Yeah, you can get a summons out of class, or if you ditch classes, you have a friend of yours that's working in the office, doing the attendance, you could walk in with them doing attendance, you go to your class, erase your name as absent, you're present.

Casper told of being sent to the office with a referral for a friend.

> So what I did was, my other friend came, he was walking with another kid, I was all, "Here," I knew he would have done it, I was like, "Here, go give this to the office."

> He was all scared and he threw it in the trash can and I went back to class. I was like, "I gave it to Joey to go get to the office, cuz I didn't want to walk down there." She's all, "Why did you give it to him?" She thought he took it and he never got called in, and she thought he did.

Several students habitually skipped class if they were already tardy or ditched school instead of going to the office with a referral. Casper learned to avoid detention at his previous school by taking advantage of the policy that students fill out their own detention slip and keep a copy for themselves. He discovered how to sign the pressure-sensitive slip so that only the first copy was legible. Although he appeared to be complying with the teacher's request, he kept the the first page and the office and referring teacher were left with blank forms.

At his old school, Casper also enjoyed getting away with a late entry to class:

> Sometimes I'd just like, cuz kids would be all up and standing around, and teacher didn't know who's there, so I'd be in my class and then everybody's be standing, so I'd sneak in and sit down. And they wouldn't know who sat down or not. So I'd be there.

Proctors can be used to effectively manipulate the system. In order to leave campus without being observed, students closely monitor the proctors' schedules. Chatting with a proctor long enough to be late to class provided the student with an excuse for missing some boring class time. It is also fun to hoodwink the proctors. Rebecca explained:

> Or sometimes, like, you need a pass, to go to the restroom and stuff like that. Sometimes you can make your own pass and just walk around. And then like, the proctors, they see you twice again, and they'll ask you, like, "What are you still doing here?" You go, we'll say like, "Well, that bathroom was locked, or didn't have any paper, so we went over here to go get the, see if there was any paper there, or if not, there's no paper over there," but we're really walking around or something.

Students with a good reputation could leave school early by walking confidently past the proctors and out the gate. But Robert complained, "Some of the proctors let you leave. . . . But, I mean, when they let you leave, that's no fun." Instead, he preferred to

> send somebody to go talk to a proctor, tell the proctor, "Hey, there's somebody over here, doing this." Proctor turns around, walks that way, and you walk right behind the proctor, out the gate . . . to get by the proctor, or like that, it was just like a big game, pretty much.

Actually, Robert said, after he successfully got away from the campus, it gets boring. During the day, nothing . . . You can't go out, school police sees you, you're in trouble. Now if they see and you run from them, now that's fun. You have them chasing you and they're pissed off like hell. But they can't hit you . . .

Johnny agreed that "running away from proctors, you know, that's fun." He gleefully recounted a story of escaping the proctors by jumping over the school fence. Unfortunately, he was recognized and was assigned one day in the ABC room when he returned to school.

Carla tried to get kicked out of a boring class once, but, "I had to do it [misbehave] and do it over, until I got suspended for a week." But she said that some of her friends

like messing around too much. They'll mess around for a while, and then they'll keep on doing it until they get in trouble. And sometimes they just do it because they want to get in trouble and get kicked out of the classroom.

Having Fun

Although she complained about not learning enough in school, Carla, too, enjoyed fooling around in class:

And they used to do a lot of things in there. They used to make the trash cans get on fire, and they used to do a lot of weird things. And it's funny. And it's always funny, cuz they would always pick on Mr. Smith. Like, um, they would throw trash cans against the wall, then they would go like that, and it was always funny. But then Mr. Smith, he used to, he used to laugh with them, because it's funny. But sometimes he used to get mad, and they'd keep on doing it until Mr. Smith said, "No, you guys don't get out, I'm gonna call the proctor." And the guys would say, "No, no, no! All right, all right, we won't do it, we won't do it!" And they would sit down and they would start throwing papers and keep on doing things, you know? And I liked that class, because we never did nothing, and I got used to it. And we never did nothing in that class. . . . He was my best teacher!

Casper successfully hid sunflower seeds in the typewriter during the regular Friday searches at his old school.

Outsmarting adults can also be a school survival skill, as when Casper was told by the disciplinarian that his friends had accused him of throwing the stink bomb. He realized he was being lied to and warned his friends not to fall for that trick.

Casper said sometimes he just wanted to give his teachers a hard time, because otherwise, "there'd be no fun in going to school." But he recognized some boundaries and worried about respecting them:

A lot of people think metal detectors and all of these things they're getting in schools, that's gonna help, but . . . they might have metal detectors at the front gate and stuff, but a kid could always have a friend go in with no weapon or nothing, then go to the back gate, when no one's around, and then hand them a gun, couple of guns or something, then the other kid is gonna go through the metal detector, how can they get busted or stuff? That's not really helping. Or it's like, it's just more challenge for the kid to get in. And they'll be like, "Well, let's see if we can get something in today," and it's the challenge, cuz when someone says, "You can't bring this, or you're gonna get busted," like Walkmans you can't bring, people are like, "Well, we're gonna bring them in our bag anyway, it's like . . . Well, let's see if we can get past all this," or hop over the fence or something, or throw them over the fence and then go pick them up or something. It's easy, like it can be done at any school. Unless you have a brick wall all around it, which you're not going to have. Slip them under the gate . . .

This issue seemed to concern Casper, because he would have to deal with a conflict that was serious to him. He firmly believed that guns and drugs do not belong in school, but feared he would have to bring them in as a response to the challenge of getting around adult restrictions.[1]

Getting Away with It

Very few people enjoy negative consequences, even if those are limited to a frown or a lecture. Students value adults' respect, especially their parents' and may take action to ensure that they keep it. Even those who do not do well in school are intelligent, and, as a part of "the game" and for other reasons, work hard to circumvent school discipline procedures.

Although she respected her parents highly, Rebecca sometimes deceived them:

Like, the second my report card [arrives], sometimes I look, [and if] my parents are gonna say something [bad], . . . I get to the mail first, I get it, and I throw it, the report card, away. I look at it, unless if it's good grades, I'll let them see it. But if there are bad grades and if they show like how many days I've been absent, or how many times I haven't been to that class and all that stuff, that's the part I don't want them to see. So, I just throw it away, so they don't see it. And then I guess, the teachers send a letter home, saying I'm failing class, I'll just get it and throw it away. Or like that. And, but sometimes, I need to get something signed for the teacher, I just do it myself. I probably do it myself.

Other students got excuses from parents, convinced family members to sign forms without reading them, and had adult relatives telephone teachers to avoid parent contact. They also erased teacher messages from the telephone answering

---

[1]Samples and Aber (1998) report that metal detectors deter, but do not prevent, guns from being brought into schools.

machine and disconnected the telephone on evenings they expected a teacher to call home.

A Teacher's View

Preservice teachers, adults outside of schools, and some within, often assume that adolescents automatically obey teachers. If there is a conflict, they believe it is the result of confusion, and a well-organized discussion or a sermon from an authority figure will effect the desired behavior.

Freddie was one of those students who just drove me mad. He had a good heart and tried hard, in spite of many academic disabilities. His humor was irrepressible, and he was often spontaneously and effectively kind to a student who needed human caring (this was while I was being a professional educator instead of a real teacher). Nonetheless, he was totally unable to align his own behavior with school and class rules. Before a field trip, we went over the rules.

"Freddie, " I asked, "have we forgotten anything?"

"Yes, Ms. T. No smoking on the bus."

"Right. In fact, no smoking anywhere. Right, Freddie?"

"Right! No smoking anywhere, for you either, Ms. T."

Fifteen minutes later, as we barreled toward the city, I smelled smoke. I looked back and there, way in the back of the bus, surrounded by a cloud of smoke, sat Freddie. I stomped back to his seat. "Freddie! What is the rule about smoking?"

Dead serious, he exhaled and replied, "*No smoking,* Ms. T. Not on the bus, and not anywhere else. No smoking today."

Calmly I wondered aloud, "Why are you smoking, Freddie?"

Freddie, too, looked as if he was wondering; wondering if I've lost my mind. "I'm not smoking," he answered.

I envisioned a burnt hand, or a lit cigarette rolling under the seat to smolder and explode. "Put the cigarette out and don't let me see any more smoke within five yards of you." So he did, and I didn't.

We had these conversations many times, about talking, fighting, throwing, and other misbehaviors. Punishment, understanding, humor, nothing I did had an effect. Freddie could quote the rules, discuss the reason for them, identify good and bad behaviors in other students, but never seemed to connect them to himself.

Most students do understand what they're doing, but may not perceive it in the same way that an adult does. They have also learned, too often, that adults, including and especially those they meet in school, have an unrealistic view of the world. It is not always practical to behave in the way educators recommend. Sometimes it's because many adolescents believe themselves to be invincible. Other times, sadly, it is because they know only too well how vulnerable they are. Today I am grateful that no one seemed to take my naive comments about gangs, guns, and everyone being friends seriously. Doing so could have resulted in injury or death.

Somehow, I always thought that what I said mattered. Often it did, especially when I said the wrong thing. My most earnest lectures, discussions, didactic lessons, however, seemed to be ignored. Oh, smart students will smile, nod, and even rephrase and role-play adult wisdom, but they will apply only what is sensible in their view of the world. Don't you?

Sometimes it seemed as if we were all playing a game. Students tried to get away with behaviors, through subterfuge, argument, or strategy. Although the students I talked to vehemently denied malicious intent, I was often convinced that my students shared a desire to drive me crazy.

Class size, administrative procedures, and distracted teachers are all fodder for students with a bent for mischief. Teachers and administrators get caught up in "the game," too. One tactic is to kick a difficult student out of the room for the least infraction, thus avoiding potential disruptions. The administrative parallel is to get habitual troublemakers to drop out of school by suspending them so frequently that it becomes impossible to keep up with class work.

Students' definitions of "fun" and "play" in the classroom also include new knowledge, challenges, interesting activities, and active engagement. Well-planned lessons can significantly decrease the students' need for disruptive "fun," but, in my experience, prom plans, a really good joke, and outside frustrations will still interfere with the teaching learning process.

Meeting Students' Needs

> *Like, since I started going to high school, I was like, . . . "I'm gonna drop out, watch I'm gonna drop out." . . . And I was all, "Why, why? What's the big thing about dropping out? I don't have to go to school; I don't have to listen to teachers; I don't have to do homework; I don't have to do nothing."*
>
> —Carla

Schools have tried to recognize the fundamental differences between students' lives and their academic needs for decades. The "ivory tower" created centuries ago to encourage contemplation and philosophy isn't very useful to more practical learners, but we still have difficulty connecting the realities of modern life with academic practice. Students who evaluated their schools with a grade of C or less reported "a lack of interesting and relevant classes, little personalized instruction, and more discipline problems" (Cromer, 1997, p. 13).

When I began teaching, I followed the textbook carefully. Teacher's guides were gospel to me. If I didn't know the answer, or couldn't find it, then the question was moot. I was *in control*. The more I tried to maintain control, the more the students tried to wrest it from me (and they were right—I really didn't know much!) Soon, class time alternated between my droning lectures and their devious detours, all leavened by the occasional carefully constructed multiple choice/essay test, which many failed. Fortunately, at that time I had the luxury of teaching in a small, private, international day school in which the students were unfailingly courteous with above average academic skills. They were too polite to totally destroy me, and too well behaved for me to blame them for my failures. I had to look at myself, my teaching, and my curriculum. *I* had to change! With the help of colleagues, research, and most of all the students, I slowly began to grow into a more student-centered teacher. Somehow, the more I relinquished control and discipline, the fewer problems I had. As we explored their questions and interests, I discovered that we were reconstructing the traditional curriculum, with a few changes, and at a much more rigorous academic level. Deadly grammar lessons became intriguing puzzles to solve and led to tentative explorations of linguistics. If I couldn't provide answers to their questions, we searched them out together. Behavior ceased to be an issue, unless I stopped listening.

Of course, those were "good" kids, ideal really. The school was, in many ways, a recreation of the ivory tower, isolated from the community at large. When I moved to a more normal public school, with children from working class rather than executive parents, in a special education room, where bad behavior was the expectation, I quickly moved back to my control stance, administering a carefully constructed, well-researched curriculum of fun, easy worksheets, and dealing with the problems using positive reinforcement whenever possible. Whatta dummy! Eventually I got tired of juggling our increasingly complex point system, frustrated by the lack of progress the students were making, and gradually reverted to more student-centered approaches. Of course, we still had problems, but again, the less I controlled, the more controlled the class became. Behavior and academics improved beyond all expectations. I guess part of respecting students is respecting their abilities and interests, even though they do not fit traditional academic molds.

Turning over Control

In a traditional program, expanding curriculum and changing teaching methods means the teacher has to make decisions about what to retain, what to add, when and how to teach, and how to evaluate. These changes require a lot of research, learning, and changing as the teacher begins to move outside of previously learned material. Frankly, there just isn't time. I solved the time question by ceding some more control to the learners.

At the beginning of the year, I reminded my students that we were in school for a particular learning purpose. I referred them to the table of contents in the text or an outline of the school curriculum plan for the subject and content we were supposed to cover. Together, we blocked out a calendar for the year, deciding how much time to spend on each area or unit. Then I asked, "What else do we need to learn this year? What do you want to learn?" We decided how many additional group or independent units we wanted to include and went back to fit them into the calendar. Students always wanted to "party" and take field trips, so we also decided which particular accomplishments we wanted to celebrate and how. Field trips were difficult on our school budget, so we usually ended up planning optional Saturday excursions. No, we never completed the work we scheduled, but we made more progress with fewer disruptions than with my previous teacher/text-centered methods.

We organized activities and units in what I have since learned is called KWL. After announcing the topic, I asked the students to brainstorm what they already knew (K). I had pictures, books, and references to movies and television programs ready in case they didn't think they knew anything. This conversation led into a discussion of what they wanted to know and how they could learn it (W). At first, I then identified what I would teach them, but later, and more effectively, I participated more actively in the design of questions and set my own learning goals along with the class. Finally, we decided how we could best demonstrate our learning (L). This was usually in the form of a written paper, but sometimes, especially with individual projects, it was through a public sharing of information so that everyone could learn. Peer revision and peer editing of written work, cooperative learning activities, and small group discussions also ensured that information was shared.

Well. Learning increased phenomenally, both in quantity and quality. Students began to have "fun" "playing" with information and ideas. Yes, they got off track, and sometimes got out of control, but behavior was generally much improved. Additionally, adult skills of interaction and self-discipline developed in a natural way. My job changed from dispensing information and controlling attention to locating resources, coordinating activities, and modeling a variety of learning techniques.

Although students explored topics relating to individual interests and backgrounds, it was relatively easy to frame them in reference to district curricula. Indeed, since most materials are written within the framework of the dominant culture, it is sometimes difficult to avoid constructing knowledge in the prescribed way. Besides, most students know what they're "supposed" to be learning and want to know what their peers know and what employers or postsecondary education programs require.

What the Research Says Will Work

Research is beginning to document the practical value of respectful theory. Offering more intense or longer experiences that will duplicate earlier education rarely helps students catch up. We need to diversify schools to meet diverse learning needs and provide more care and engagement to improve failing schools and students (Raywid, 2001). Although referring to higher education, Rouner's (1993) comments pertain equally to secondary education in the Information Age:

The current curriculum debate tends to miss the point because the critical question . . . is not primarily information, but transformation. The test is less how much students know, of whatever cultural tradition, because they are going to forget most of that content in five years. The test is who a student has become in that [educational] process. In other words, "What have they made of you?" (p. 141)

A change in educational goals requires many changes in the education process. Crews and Counts (1997) suggest, "There needs to be continued study to determine what efforts can be made by the larger society to assist schools in being more effective, rather than what schools can do to assist the larger society" (p. 138). We need much more research on the effects of improved curriculum, school attributes, teacher attitude, and improved communication among teachers, students, and parents.

Current research implies that effective small group work is the best way to promote intergroup relations among students (Weiner, 1999). It also helps us manage diverse interests, abilities, and personalities in large classes and encourages students to remain engaged.

Pares and Pares (2001) list strategies for teachers to increase self-regulated learning among students. Everyone in the class needs to learn to analyze style and evaluate knowledge. The learning process itself should periodically be assessed by the individual and the group. Students need to practice setting goals, managing resources (especially time), and reviewing and revising learning. Although self-regulated learning is an individual process, learners should also participate in the learning community.

The philosophies of critical pedagogy[2] have helped me think about schooling and frame questions and concerns about what I saw. Finding information about specific cultures both to guide my interactions and to teach multiple views of history and literature seemed to be an insurmountable task until I remembered to ask and listen. Strange though it seems, students learn more if they participate in the construction and delivery of units. Helping the class identify questions and locating answers enabled us to collect and process much more information about multiple points of view, included each student's interest area, and involved them too completely to allow for serious misbehavior. They also learned a greater percentage of the material required by the district than when I relied on textbooks and my expertise alone.

[2]Paolo Freire, Peter McLaren, and John Ogbu are some writers who raise critical questions about monocultural education in a multicultural world.

Results

Noise and disorder are part of the classroom, according to John Dewey and other student-centered educators. Minor infractions of traditional discipline codes do occur more often when classroom activities and structure are loosely defined: Teacher-led small groups are more orderly than independent, open classes; restricted movement, spelling tests, worksheets, and other predictable activities are orderly; open spaces, student choice, complex tasks such as word problems and essays tend to be disorderly (Gottfredson et al., 1993).

Discipline standards, then, must be adapted to changing pedagogies. Excited learners *are* "disorderly" when measured against rules for teacher-controlled, passive learning activities. Part of the process of moving toward student-centered learning is helping youngsters find effective ways to share their discoveries and excitement without disrupting others' learning. Another factor to understand is the value of leaving the assigned topic to discuss something else, either to rest one's mind or to clear the head of more pressing issues. Finally, it is critical to recognize the importance to conceptual development of staring into space, quiet abstraction, and solitary muttering.

The prevention of violent behavior is a function, not of constraining discipline procedures, but of the social environment of schools, including the policies and practices of an administration and faculty that support and encourage a positive learning environment (Hawkins, Farrington, & Catalano, 1998).

Perry and Duke (1978) explain that small size, flexibility, and teacher-student relations minimize discipline problems in alternative schools. One program put students who were identified as having behavior problems into relaxation sessions, magic circle activities, art, future planning, and decision-making classes; created a system of checks for misbehavior and points for good behavior; arranged counseling sessions for the students; and held training programs for the teachers. Students improved behavior, attendance, motivation, and self-concept, while teachers became more knowledgeable in program planning and intervention techniques (Mills, 1987).

An urban high school, after experiencing serious discipline problems and teacher frustration, created an evening school alternative to suspensions and expulsions. There, in a maximum five-week assignment, students work on academics with teachers, but also work on their own problems in small groups led by a counselor or other support staff. This approach, combined with an academy program during the day, led to significant improvements in attendance, academic behavior, and morale (McPortland, Jordan, Legters, & Balfanz, 1997).

Some schools are moving more aggressively to change children's understanding of themselves and the world. One school has implemented a K–12 social/emotional learning curriculum designed by parents, teachers, administrators, and community members. They report reduced feelings of fear, fewer incidents of gun and knife carrying, and improved attitudes toward the school and community among the students (Sullivan, DeCarlo, DeFalco, & Roberts, 1998).

Cross-age tutoring is one method used to build adolescent confidence, self-control, social skills, and sense of responsibility. It does, in fact, reduce truancy and tardiness (Lazerson, Foster, Brown, & Hummel, 1988). Other service learning activities can be used for the same purposes and to build specific employment skills. Many of these activities help students connect school requirements and academic learning with requirements and knowledge needed to function in the adult world.

Remember, however, that " A focus on self-determination leads inevitably to the need to consider personal and personally valued outcomes for students . . ." (Wehmeyer & Schalock, 2001, p. 15). In other words, traditional school curricula and academic valued may no longer be appropriate.[1]

Flexible scheduling, changed behavioral standards, shifting centers of control, variable curricula, and other classroom and institutional adjustments will result in a different kind of schooling. When you set up your classroom so that students respect and learn from each other, and you learn from them, you contradict the hierarchical nature of the school system. When you use teaching strategies that call for your students to interpret and analyze materials so that you and they can critically compare ideas, you counter the "skill – drill – kill" sort of instruction that lends itself to the test-driven curricula that characterize many urban schools (Weiner, 1999, p. 61).

We saw bits of it as we changed our class procedures. It was messy, unpredictable, and exciting. The students learned more of the canon than they had under previous conditions; discipline problems were redefined; they acquired improved self-management skills, adult social skills, and supportive interactive skills. The strongest image I remember is the start of surprise when the final bell rang, as opposed to our usual habits of waking up and winding down five minutes before the end of the period.

Some Activities to Try

As we begin to speak openly, there is an increase in debate, the defense of "right" and "wrong" answers, and discomfort with developing confusion. Students become angry and frustrated with me, with their peers, and with themselves.

Everyone Talks: For a whole group discussion of the chapter, seat the students in rows or small groups. No student can speak a second time until everyone in that row or group has spoken once. A participation grade is based on the number of contributions each group makes to the discussion. Students may help each other with answers to questions, ideas on contributions, and so on.

Helping Colleagues: Ask students to raise their hands for any subject they hated in high school. Call out the content areas represented by the students in the class. In content area groups, have the students meet with someone who hated their

---

[1]Agran (1997) discusses ways to help students with severe cognitive or emotional deficits work toward self-determination.

content and find out why, collect stories about their experiences, and further explore. As a class, brainstorm a list of reasons students do not enjoy certain subjects.

Quick Write: Write a letter to convince someone your class has value.

Cooperative Learning: In small groups, with mixed content areas, have students create graphic organizers of theories of education or content area information.

Research: Students who are interested in continuing their academic development, have other questions to ask adolescents, or realize that the Southern California urban high schoolers have different reactions and perceptions than teens in their community can do a pilot research project to find out what local students believe. For my sanity and student growth, I assign the project in parts:

1. Like any other teacher, you have to do several things at once, especially at the beginning of a research project. These are the parts of the project and their due dates. You will need to work on several parts simultaneously to complete the project on schedule.

   a. Qualitative researchers must identify themselves and their biases. (Due date in one or two weeks) write 1 to 3 pages identifying yourself, your experiences in high school, especially with your topic, and your assumptions about your findings.

   b. (Due date in two to four weeks) write a proposal for your project that addresses a specific topic relating to (course title). The proposal should identify the topic, explain its importance, and list several resources available to you for background information. You should also explain how you will get information in your school (what questions will you ask, how will you get responses, etc.). Before submitting the proposal, you must have approval for the project from the superintendent and principal of the school you are going to investigate.

   c. For (due date about halfway through the semester) write a review of the current literature on your topic. By now you should also have permission from the people you are going to talk with and, for students, permission from their parents and the classroom teacher.

   d. For (due date after about two-thirds of the semester) summarize your findings in the school.

   e. For (due in the following week or two) write your conclusions, describe their applicability, identify future research plans.

   f. For (due the penultimate class) revise your paper as needed. Go back to your proposal and rewrite it in the past tense, explaining any changes in procedure or affects of your assumptions. It becomes the "methods" section of your research. Write a 250-word abstract for your portfolio. Present your findings to the class and lead a discussion about them.

2. I use a writing process approach and create class time for brief small group meetings. Students have to have two classmates sign off on each section before submitting it to me.

This format is also useful for content area research. The schedule and specific requirements should be adapted to the needs of the teacher and the program.

Teaching Opportunities: This would be a good time for students to teach management techniques based on behavioral theory or to lead a discussion on the pros and cons of these methods. Other students can identify topics on student-centered learning and schedule a time to teach them. In high school, presentations should begin halfway through the unit so that there are only one or two each day. That way, students don't get bored, but do have a change to process the information and integrate knowledge from various sources into their own understanding.

Part IV

Endings

The end of the school year is an odd time. Normally, good students are passing, have been accepted for jobs or postsecondary programs, and have made plans for Life After School. Often, they quit working after spring break or the senior prom. They want to relax and be entertained, but they're willing to exert themselves to provide the fun if you won't do it. The normally difficult students are frantically trying to inch their grades up a notch, working hard, and demanding more. The really bad students have disappeared.

As we moved into student-centered programming, these problems faded as students finished their projects, set new goals, and sadly said goodbye for the summer. We still had some behavior problems, but they weren't as bad as before, nor did we get as frustrated. There were no dropouts, but there was some pretty wild scrambling and wheeling and dealing for grades. Additionally, there were more and more incredibly wonderful times when we were a learning community: a group of people exploring, arguing, challenging, sharing, supporting, laughing, and growing together.

Our wonderful times were measured in moments, occasional class periods, but never even a full day. Sometimes students grew into these phases independently or in pairs or small groups of friends. Individual student growth lasted longer and seemed to affect learning more deeply. In our small community, friendships had been well established since the third or fourth grade. Troublemakers banded together to dodge learning, while academic students enjoyed each other's company, but learned on their own. As we changed the way we taught, students changed the way they interacted with each other. CHS students valued their friendships, but their relationships did not always help each other learn. How did they perceive socialization in school? What contributed to the sometimes violent, uncontrolled interactions at CHS?

Sometimes a student came to us with an established independent learning style, which we enjoyed fostering; more often students came to the class with poor behavior and discouraged, passive/resistant learning habits, so that we had to spend most of the year undoing past experiences and teaching/modeling new ways to learn. We had to use behavioral techniques to get them started with academics and to teach them *how* to succeed and to live with success. Then we had to practice democratic procedures, respectful discussions, consensus building, information sharing, and other skills important in the type of community we wanted. We had to do what they wanted, in spite of our better judgement. Usually things worked out okay.

Expanding the curriculum to meet student needs meant changing teaching practice and expanding resources. The walls of the classroom began to disappear, the school and expert hierarchies had to relinquish some authority, and faculty thinking had to become less rigid and more imaginative. It wasn't always easy. Classroom management problems didn't disappear, or even decrease, but they changed, to focus on monitoring and facilitating student growth.

The results were, I think, wonderful. Instead of dropping out, students were graduating and even going on to a variety of postsecondary programs. Most found employment, and some, after a few years, opened their own successful businesses. When they dropped in to say hello and show off family pictures, they also asked if I had seen the most recent PBS presentation of *Lear*, or talked of a trip to the mountains with a loved one and Robert Frost. They were curious explorers of and responsible contributors to the adult world.

7

Friendship and Peer Interaction

*. . . Just do things like, to make their friends think that, aw yeah, he's all right,
cuz he can get in trouble, he's not afraid, he's not afraid of an adult.*

—Rebecca

Researchers, parents, and other adults often blame a student's choice of friends for misbehavior. Youngsters who join gangs are commonly believed to be led astray by them. Worse than the individual troublemaker or class clown is the group of friends who egg each other on.

Tom pointed out that sometimes kids break rules to impress their peers or as a result of being dared to do something, but friends and peers were usually only briefly mentioned as being a reason to misbehave. Ana did not want to associate with many of the students at CHS and implied that she felt personally unsafe.

Getting in Trouble

Carla told of how her friends pushed her into fighting, to maintain the group standard of personal honor.

Casper, perhaps because his friends were so far away, discussed them most frequently. Like many students, he felt his friends got him in trouble, either through subterfuge or by leading him to break rules.

In his old school, Casper and his friends would, "just out of fun . . . Turn out the lights, and throw a desk over, no one . . . knows who did it . . ." He also talked about more complex schemes:

> . . . there's been days when the kid's been gone, like two kids will be out of that class, and everybody's perfect, and then the teacher will be, "Yeah, those two kids are gone,

so everybody's perfect." But when those kids, the next day, everything goes up again. Starts back up . . . It's not really the two kids, but like when two kids are gone, then there's only so many kids in the class, so we're not gonna cause anything. And when there's two gone, it'd be even obvious if we start something, cuz they'll know it's out of us three.

Getting friends in trouble added to the humor:

> One time, my friend . . . got in trouble for something and he got sent to the office and then everybody in the class was good. He's (the teacher) all like, "Yeah, see . . ." and everybody's like, "Yeah, it's always Duncan's fault. He's causing it all." And the teacher's like, "Yeah, everybody's good now." And then the teacher's like, "Yeah, I'm gonna try to get him out of here!" And then he heard him like yeah, they're all saying after you left everybody's good, trying to get you out of there and stuff.
>   . . . Then, like when someone's like, when he comes back, kids would start up again. "See, it's always your fault." Then he'd get in trouble. Kids have it planned too. Like sometimes I'd be like, I wouldn't be in yet. And right when he'd walk back in they'd all start talking; he'd be talking too. And they'd send him out again and everybody'd be like, mmmmmm doing their work. But then the other kids, they'd start blaming it on other kids too when they'd be out, like, "Oh, it's always them two, or them two." So whenever there's a group, there's always big trouble.

Casper and his friends knew that they had to behave in a small group, because it was too difficult to get away with anything.

Casper also wanted to avoid becoming involved with a "bad" group at CHS, so that he could stay out of trouble. Sometimes his old friends tricked the teacher into believing he had done something wrong.

> Oh yeah. Well, like there'll be a kid, like messing around, playing with the typewriter, and when she says stop, he'll be like, "It wasn't me!" And there'll just be one kid in there, and he'll be like, "It wasn't him, it was *him!*" Try to blame someone else, so then he'll get sent out. And then that's what happened to me one time.
>   I was going to throw trash away, and then one of them would flick off the lights and I got blamed for it. I was like, "I didn't" and there was a substitute too. They had it planned.

Other times:

> . . . like down there I have all my friends, and like one time we'd say, "Let's leave, let's ditch." And I was like, "All right, fine, it's only PE." And PE I didn't really like, cuz I've, the grade was, didn't pass PE. And it's the easiest thing, but we'd leave.
>   But it's like, different things too. Cuz when I was down there, with all my friends, like everybody that I knew. And they're all like, " Come on, let's do this." "No, I don't want to." "Oh come on." "All right, fine, let's turn off the lights." "You turn off the lights!" And, of course, I'd go over there and flip the light off.
>   If I'm with, that I know, like my friends down there, they'll say something and, "OK, let's do it. I'll be a part of it." We'll all have it planned out, like when there's a

substitute. One time I was involved. There was a substitute, and like the teacher's aide always goes out to use the restroom after second period, so right when she walks out, one of the kids'll flip off the light, or we'll have it planned. And then one of the kids distracted the substitute; I was at the light switch; the kid hit it off and then desks went flying over, typewriters went, a glass glitter bottle went flying and got glitter all over everybody and hit right on the microwave, busted the whole bottle; then I was like, I didn't get busted that time, cuz I had it planned, I was sitting down and stuff. Cuz I was like, I was talking, "Yeah, uh, . . . I need help with this one problem." And she was looking, she was over there looking and the lights flipped off. I was supposed to get her distracted. And it worked out.

Aware of the reputation he and his friends had acquired in his previous school, Casper was anxious to avoid problems at CHS:

Cuz like whenever a kid would get in trouble, sometimes I'd be sitting next, and I'd go out with him, getting searched. And they throw stink bombs in the class, and I'd be out there getting searched.

[Now it's] a new environment; it's a new start. And I don't want the reputation I've got down there, where all the teachers say, "Yeah, that's Casper. Look out for him. He's always getting in trouble." But up here, if I show a good impression now, it'll be like, "Well that kid is new here, but I don't know if he'll get in trouble. But down there he did, but up here he's a pretty good kid." That's how I want it to be. Because it's a different environment.

Casper was the product of a punitive, controlling system of management. His special education program was also watered down, frequently consisting of games and videos. He and his friends responded by figuring out how to get around the system, disrupt an unproductive education plan, and create their own challenges. His previous response to gun control fits into this picture and suggests to me that he is preparing for an adult role as a good-natured petty criminal.

Casper was placed in the new school, about an hour's drive from his home community, as a result of a court decision and his mother's move. His choice was to shape up or be moved to a detention center. He seemed to be frightened and motivated by these actions. What would happen if he and his friends were challenged to solve a content-related problem they found interesting? Would they work together as well to invent an egg cushion or matchstick bridge as they did to plant stink bombs and evade detection?

Peer Responsibility

In contrast, Alissa and Don spoke of their role in helping their friends improve. Alissa wanted to be a good example for her classmates:

I hope by my attitude that I can influence people around me; if they're my age or my friends who might be acting rowdy or whatever. I hope that they can look at me and settle down a little bit. You know, just try and be a good example for every people; not necessarily to walk around and say, "Oh well, look at me. I'm doing this and that!" But, just hold myself, the way I carry myself and be a good person.

Don also saw a responsibility to be a role model for his peers:

My job as a student is to do my work, be the best I can be, make other people look at me and want to try to be like me, you know, do the things I do. Like if they see, like, say you used to be a bad person, and then all of a sudden, you change yourself around, and like, you're doing good. So then, like the people that's still being bad, they'll look at you like, "Aw, you used to be bad like me. So now, I think I want to get like that, and be smart." Have a little sense, you know.
    . . . I'm trying to follow it through . . . leave a good footprint there, another person can follow.

Don and Alissa have more socially acceptable goals and behaviors. They want to position themselves as "experts" in the student hierarchy and show other students how to behave. They are certainly ready to become tutors and peer mediators. How is the school fostering their social development? Do peer leadership programs interfere with academic growth? What kinds of relationships are encouraged? Are these students ready to assume cooperative roles in group learning, or will they be hindered by their need to be leaders?

Even though the teachers trust in the students' sense of responsibility, the students will mess around, sometimes inappropriately. We all need to have fun and we spend a lot of time in school. How can we make school more fun for all of us without interfering with the educational process? Where do we draw the line? What do we do when students cross it?

Although the students didn't particularly support it, researchers and common wisdom assign friendship groups an important, usually negative, role in the growing up process. These teenagers told stories of getting into trouble with and because of their friends, but also talked about being supported by them, learning from them, and trying to help them grow. How can we encourage the strong points of friendship? Can we help our students help their friends? Is it possible to develop acquaintance and collegial skills rather than encouraging the friend/enemy dichotomy?

The Riots

Students often referred to a series of lunch hour disturbances, called riots by most members of the campus community, as we discussed discipline issues. These discussions brought out several seminal connections between school, community, discipline, and safety as perceived by students.

How do classroom management procedures affect campus interactions? How do administrators contribute to the learning environment? What influence does the outside community have on school social structures?

Some people blamed the fight Johnny spoke of earlier,[1] others saw no connections. But it is clear that something exploded during the first semester and continued to foment during the entire school year. The first episode was shocking and frightening; the violence resulted in injuries to students. Ana called her husband to come and get her:

> Cuz everybody, you could just see everybody running from where we were at, you know, the last time we were up there eating, everybody coming down. All, there was, the office, all the doors, they were packed. People were running out the doors, crossing the street, waiting for their parents, you know, there was parents up there, because everybody was . . .

Robert finished, "I mean, she called me, I was there before City PD was there. I mean, I was leading the pack. I had all these cops behind me." When he arrived and saw "the kids calling, telling their friends, 'Bring me my gun; I want my gun.' What is that?" He shook his head in dismay.

The students believed that the first riot was started by a fight between a Mexican and an African American over a nonracial issue. When the fighting escalated, the combatants took sides by race. Rebecca explained:

> I think it was just they had a little racial thingy there, but, I heard that what started the whole fight were that two people, two freshmen, all they were doing was fighting. I guess like, you know, that person gets his home boys, and then that guy gets his home boys, right, and then they started fighting all together. And they think it's like a gang war, and then they start saying racial things. And it ends up like a racial thing . . . So everybody just starts fighting, when they feel a whole crowd fighting, well, everybody joins in. So some people just want to fight cuz they want to fight.

The following semester there was another riot. Carla explained, "I think they just, it's just to fight. Like the last one, the last one we had. . . . some guy from ____ Street [a Mexican gang] killed a Black [gang member] from here and they got mad . . ."

Chaquan gave another version:

> No, I'm not around, but I saw . . . it was . . . they started throwing apples and stuff. . . . It was the Mexicans against the Blacks. But most of these people, they don't listen to the teachers, cuz they told them to go back to class, and they didn't go. And then they was asking questions on what's gonna happen when we walked home, would we be jumped or whatever . . .
>
> This one girl, she wanted to know, cuz she had a baby and she walks home with the stroller. And he [the principal] was like, "We don't care." And they tried to spray some Mace in her eyes cuz she wanted to go to the day care to see her baby. (*The security people?*) They had the police department up there . . . she wanted to go see her baby and they tried to spray her with some Mace. (*Was she going into the riot,*

---

[1]See page 44.

or?) No, she was trying to go around, out the front gate, so she could go to the day care. They're (the teachers and security personnel) like, "You can't go. Your baby's all right." She didn't believe them. And everybody got mad about that. Cuz there's a lot of girls up there that want, that have babies and want to go see them.

I don't think, they didn't let anybody off campus. If you would have gone off campus, you would have went as soon as the riot started, cuz they locked all the gates. . . . They thought that was going to make us go back to class, but it didn't. Cuz it just got people madder. Cuz I wanted to go home, but they locked the gates.

The security guards and proctors were unable to control the students. Johnny described one incident:

And then they were throwing trashcans at him, and then some guy shanked on him, with a pencil or something, and then like, it wasn't true. Because he was just grabbing people just for nothing. He just grabbed a Mexican and threw him in the back and then there's another guy, he got angry, and he said, "You better leave my home boy alone!" He went straight up to him and started socking him, and the police grabbed him, the police grabbed him, "Come on, come on, you're under arrest." And they arrested my friend, it wasn't fair, because, another friend got away. Except another friend, my other friend got arrested cuz he tried to help him, and then he got arrested. So my other friend, he didn't get arrested yet, so we were going down there by the parking lot, the principal grabbed him and said, "Come here. You're under arrest." "Yeah, right. What'd I do? I didn't do anything." Cuz he was pushing the cop. And he says, "So what? The cop was pushing me."

Carla described the ending:

Everybody was like running around. The teachers were, really controlled it. Like they took all of the Mexicans on one side and all the Blacks on the other. Like we're all standing over here. And some Mexicans would just want to fight, and they would go over there, and the some of the Blacks would run there, but the teachers be there.

The spring riot was, according to the students, caused by high spirits that got out of control. Chaquan summarized the beginning, "They just wanted to be doing something . . . they throw apples and milk and stuff . . . They thought we wasn't gonna (do) nothing . . . I don't think they want to get hit in the head with something . . ." Angela stayed away, but had an opinion:

Well, I think that it's just an excuse for most of the people up here to just get attention, . . . the fights just kept us from staying out of class, cuz I know a lot of people don't like to go to class anyway. So they just did this, I think they just did this just to stay out of class or something, because I mean afterwards, some people didn't even go to their classes; some people left, went home, some people went into other people's classrooms, cuz they said to go into any class you can. . . . The way the one that started, the second one that started, well, I heard that there was two Mexican girls fighting, off somewhere, and then everybody ran to watch, right? And then, when they were leaving, I heard that, I don't know if it was the Mexicans, but that's what some people said, that Mexicans started throwing apples and milk at Black people. So that's how it started. But I mean, I don't, why do you have to start something like this? I mean. Nobody was saying anything racial to anyone else, it just started. And then, when it happened like that, people started choosing sides; people started going to, Mexicans started going to the Mexicans, Black to the Black . . . you know you have friends (from other races), too. But I guess when it comes to stuff like this, they just choose their own race.

Adults interpreted the fights as race riots, but some students who talked with me did not. Alissa explained, "It's like there's some very immature people who just like to fight no matter what, and whatever reason they can use to try to justify why they're fighting, they'll use it." She saw the riots as possibly causing, rather than being the result of, racial issues:

> I think it was, if it was, you know, a Latino guy and a Black guy and they decided that they wanted to fight, for whatever reason, that they should have stayed between them two, and not to bring, you know, all your buddies in on one side and say, "Well, I'm gonna stick up for him cuz I don't like the fact that this guy is fighting him," that's one thing, but to say, "Well, he's Latino and he's Black. So Latinos think they're better, so I'm gonna get all the Black people behind me . . ." But, you know, it wasn't everybody in it, it was just one guy and he hit this other guy. And it should have stayed between them. But that's not how it was. It was, you know, it was everybody against everybody.

Carla agreed that she joined in the first riot because, "When they were jumping one of my friends, I was right there," so she entered the melee to protect her friend. She described the final riot somewhat gleefully:

> Yeah, like the last day of school was really bad, . . . It was fun and stuff, cuz everybody was throwing stuff; like everybody was throwing stuff, candy, food, and yelling and screaming and like the teachers got all mad and stuff. Like, I mean, it's not, like, I mean, it's the last day of school and stuff . . . we were just messing around . . . everybody was happy they were gonna get out of school.

He understood the amusement factor, but Tom did not take the riots so lightly:

> I was here the last riot. I was in class. I could still see what's going on. I don't like it. It's terrible. What they're doing. They're like . . . they shouldn't do it. I don't know why they start it.
> All the time I'm going to school, I've never been in a situation like this, with school. So it shocked me. Riots at school? God. First there was in L.A. that big riot, and now it's in schools everywhere! It's a shock. Oh, it's just a shock, because it shouldn't really happen like that, you know? But I don't know, I think, these riots, looks like kids are just having fun. They're just having fun with the riot. That's why they're doing it. They think it's fun just to throw things at each other, they don't care if somebody gets hurt or not. They just do it to get out of class or something. Every time they have a riot, I see my classmates and all them . . . some they go out and

participate in it too. Some of them stay in class but they watch and they kinda like, I don't know, enjoy it or something.

It's like a show. They go, "Dag, we're gonna leave early today!" They like that.

But there are also kids that are angry, too. Some of them are angry . . . First it started out as something, first it started out as a fight. It was like Blacks and Mexicans, I heard. It started out like that. And later on, kids just got in, and then it was like two groups or something. Split in Mexicans and Blacks, and they'd be like doing things, you know. First they were angry, later on they having fun, and after that, when somebody got hurt, like the two opposite participants, they would be like fighting, they would get hurt, they would get angry, during the riots. But I don't know. There was some people in it for fun, and then get angry and some people just plain alone, just having fun . . .

Although he saw the riots as a way for some students to have fun, Tom sensed an underlying anger that had potential for dangerous development.

I don't know . . . For some, they don't want to do nothing. But some, like, it's hard to fight and [be] racist when you have friends that are Black and Mexican. All united. Some of them don't want to participate. And that's good, they're united. I think they all should be united. (*Do you think that there's racism in this school?*) They don't really talk about it that much, but sometimes, I don't know, they don't really talk about it, but when it happens, it just happens.

Few of the students liked having riots at the school, but all were pessimistic about avoiding them in the future. Chaquan said the principal "went back to his office. He didn't know about anything." She stayed out of the fighting, seeing it as a temporary situation. "I didn't fight with nobody. I was just watching. I was like, I don't know why they're fighting, cuz the next week, they're gonna be friends again." She and her friends talked to the older students, who had some good ideas. Antashia commented bitterly,

They always try to say, "We're gonna prevent this from happening; we're gonna stop this from happening." We had three riots, after the first one, "We're gonna stop it from happening"; after the second one, "We're gonna stop it from happening"; the third one, "OK, this is gonna be the last, final one." You know? The final one. The first one, kids got hurt. The second one, some of them went to jail, and the third one, I don't know what happened, I was in class. They talk about doing a lot of things; stop a lot of things, but there's nothing happening.

How did the nature of the riots change as the year progressed? Why? Were the riots the result of youthful high spirits out of control or fundamental societal problems? What can we do to stop this sort of wildness? Or should we? The students had conflicting opinions. Can they be reconciled?

Friendship and peer pressure are powerful forces in adolescent society, which is centered in the schools. The usual adult reaction is to control and trivialize these relationships, but the problems continue.

How can friendships be used to help each of the students in the study group develop their academic skills? How will culture, race, class, and gender affect their interactions? What can you do, as their teacher, to foster their growth?

8

The Learning Community

We hear a lot about the "learning community." Is there such a thing? What is it? Is it confined to the classroom or the school? How important is it? Is it important at all?

School and society are closely connected. Yes, we teach children how to be citizens, but society guides what we teach, both overtly and covertly.

One problem with schools is that most teachers, administrators, and researchers have never left them. We went to kindergarten, graduated from high school, went to college, and then back to school as teachers. Except for summer jobs, most of us have had little experience with working conditions, standards, and expectations outside of the education system. Thus, our assumptions, with which we educate, direct, and discipline our students, are based on a limited life experience, one that does not necessarily parallel their own.

As educators create schools based on their understandings of life, society tries to impose wider, often different and conflicting goals on the schools. Taxpayers, school boards, real estate agents, employers, media, legislators, and other people control schooling from the outside. As a special educator, I had to coordinate sweeping legislation protecting the educational rights of children who learn differently with limited funding of a small, bedroom community, fight an antagonistic school board, and teach. Guess who lost? Every year I conferenced with each child's parents, and asked what goals we should set for their child. "Graduation, get that diploma," was their response. "What do you want your student to *learn*?" I asked. But real learning, it seemed, occurred in the home, through the union, on the job. School had little of importance to offer. Who was right? All of these tensions contributed to discipline problems.

Whether it be student self-discipline, acquired through mutual respect, discussion, and practice, or discipline imposed from the outside, based on rules and regulations, the role of discipline in the schools is no longer a matter for theoretical debate and random practice. Adolescents have relatively easy access to weapons of mass destruction, and they are using these weapons to solve their problems, in the streets and in the schools. By the time the problem comes to adult attention, maybe it is too late for punishment or counseling.

The students' talk of riots and weapons was chilling. Current events indicate their experiences are not unusual, nor are these concerns limited to one type of school. All educators need to be actively involved in the prevention of school violence. Like many secondary schools across the country, CHS has turned to security forces to protect and control their community.

Proctors and Police

They're stupid . . . They don't help anything.

—Antashia

City High School had a staff of proctors and school police officers who were responsible for apprehending students who break the rules. The students both feared and laughed at them, while occasionally establishing tentative friendly relationships.

The proctors were responsible for keeping students on campus and taking tardy students to the office. If students established a friendly relationship, some proctors would look the other way when students left or entered the campus at the wrong time. Antashia explained how they could also be used to avoid time in class:

> . . . they're just like fun; they're fun to be with. If you really know what you're doing, if you don't want to go to class, or you want to go late and just have a proctor take you to class, you could sit out here, talk to a proctor . . . He's gonna sit there and talk to you and talk to you and talk to you. By the time I get through talking, either school is out or it's halfway through your period, and he's like, "Oh, aren't you supposed to be in class?" Cuz like, "Yeah, but I don't have a pass." And he'll walk you to class, he'll be like, "Oh, she was with me."

One proctor, later dismissed, let students leave campus in exchange for drugs. They had a reputation for not breaking up fights, lest they get hit, or of arriving too late to prevent injury to one or more students. Johnny complained that as they did their job by verifying where a student should be, they were rude to the point of using their sticks on people.

Tom felt that the security force did not help the school situation because they were too strict at the wrong time.

> . . . it was the last day of school, the kids brought all this stuff, they brought water guns and all that. . . . They were like playing. The administrators . . . were saying, "Give me the water gun" and all that and kids were still more and more, all wet, . . . and it's like playing water to each other. And all you see is the security. . . . He took all the water guns away mostly, from the students, and he broke them with his stick. He broke them in front of us. He got mad! . . . So the students, oh, there was yelling! And like I said, the students wanted to go against him. . . . Students said, "Naw! I don't . . ." like they don't care no more. And they play again, and they play again.

... And he then got mad. He already warned them, you know? Take the water gun, so he got mad, he took them, he just like, "Oh yeah? You guys want to play this game, too?" He broke it. He broke like most of them that he see. He just snatched it out of there and broke it and he was mad too. He was like, stepping on it, stomping it . . . and he was real angry, stomping it and everything, and the students, all the students from CHS, they gathered around him and started yelling at him, screaming . . . all the students, just like, when he did that, mocking him. You know, like, "What the heck, break the water gun. They don't cost that much!" You know, just mocking him. And he got angry. That's why they all like, clapping. And then, luckily the students did nothing to him. I think he was mad because I think, first the students were throwing things at him too. Cuz they were bringing eggs and everything. And that's why. But I don't think he got egged, he just saw everything was thrown and he was mad.

Johnny talked about teasing school police officers. He and his friends gave one officer a nickname, which made him mad, but Johnny said that was his problem, not theirs. They tricked another officer into thinking they were using drugs on campus and when he came to investigate, they didn't have anything. As revenge, he brought a student who was on campus illegally to the office, even though the student was not misbehaving. Johnny, Robert, and Ana all laughed about running from the school police.

Johnny also talked about a friend who was suspended for five days because the school police saw that his eyes were red, although the student had not actually smoked on campus. Rebecca told of being chased by the school police in a police car when she was ditching. Carla had a friend who was put on home schooling but used to visit the campus to see her at lunch time. The police caught him and offered to protect her from him because they perceived him as being a troublemaker. They were quite insistent about getting her to accuse him of harassing her, but she refused, and tried to explain their friendly relationship. Another officer was taken to court for striking a student on the head with his club. Johnny described their relationship:

> No, I don't look at him cuz, when you look at him, he looks back at you like he's angry. Me and my friends don't like him. We don't care about him. If he comes up to me and tries to hit me, I'll kick his ass. And then like, I'll beat him up. Cuz I won't let no police hit me. Cuz I didn't do nothing wrong.

Instead of improving the school environment and making students feel safer, school police added a prison-like atmosphere to the school.

The students also had mixed feelings about the city police. Ana and her friends were picked up at a party and returned to school by the police. Her husband, however, worked with the police on a project to reduce graffiti in the city.

Although Ana and Robert were concerned about school safety, they believed too much money was spent on ineffective security. Robert said, "But look at the money they're putting in this wrought iron fence. I mean, I think the wrought iron fence was uncalled for . . . That's a prison, you know."

Alissa described the school in terms of an extended metaphor:

> This school. . . it's like a little city. Some areas have the gangsters, the upper class
> people, the brainy people, the people in between. . . . It's just like it's own little
> separate world. You came in, you're in one place, you go home, you're in another
> place. You go in the office, they're in the government . . .
>
> It's a city that definitely needs help. It needs a lot of rearranging, everything:
> attitudes, colleagues. I know we have a lot of new policies this year, but it always
> needs more of work.

How does the security system at CHS reflect security in a community populated mainly by the lower tiers of the economic system? Is CHS doing its job in preparing students to live in the existing community? What are the school community members learning about each other and their respective roles in the world? How can we ensure a physically safe place for youngsters to learn while maintaining an open environment for thinking and exploration?

Studies suggest that students seem to feel less responsibility for their peers' behavior as they move into secondary schools (Lewis, 2001). Peer mediation programs are effective in providing individualized academic instruction (Utley, 2001). Can working with, rather than under, a teacher's leadership help students improve academic and social skills?

Respect and Care

Our classroom certainly felt like a community. Two adults, an instructional assistant, and a teacher stayed in a room, and a group of about fifty teens wandered in an out for varying lengths of time. We had roles to play, jobs to do, all of which required some interaction. Like family, we squabbled, joked, and supported each other. We adults, trained to be aloof and neutral, were often in the middle of the action. We parented, befriended, advised, learned, taught, and supported, but received the same treatment from the students. (Ms. Thorson, did you study for your test tonight? It's time to take your car in for a tuneup. You work too hard, you should take some time off. *This* is how you load the projector/VCR/coffeemaker. You're late, was the ice bad? Here's a cup of hot tea.) The more communal the class became, the more students naturally helped each other and worked and learned together, the more we learned. Discipline problems became community problems, often solved before they came to adult attention (one student hisses to another, "This is *our* room, and *we* don't act that way here!").

How can we build a learning comunity? Nivek talked about student relationships at CHS: "People hate each other. They don't want to know about it, the teachers . . ." Antashia was confused about the riots and the animosity on campus: "God didn't put that much evil into anybody's heart. You know . . . that doesn't make any sense, for somebody to have that much hatred in their heart." Angela believed that

> there's a lot of disrespect in that school, toward the teachers and everybody. . . .
> Everybody doesn't really like everybody that much. That's why I think all these riots

are going on, cuz nobody has respect for anybody. . . . because well, that's what leads to fighting anyway. If you disrespect everybody else . . .

She especially worried about the way U.S. students treat teachers.

> Well, I think, I just think that we should all respect each other, because, I mean, that's the way my mom teaches me. . . . My parents are from Africa, they're from Ghana, and it's like, I don't know, I'm not just saying that this, to say something bad about Americans, I'm just saying that I think African parents are more stricter. And they teach respect. And I'm not saying that all parents in America don't, but some just leave their kids to do whatever they want to do. And my mom has taught me to respect everybody, all my elders; I know people that are older than me and stuff like that. You know how here, they have first name basis, but I can't do that. My parents told me, because I call them "uncle" or "aunt" or something like that. And it's just that I think we all need respect, to respect our elders mostly. And then our peers also. I think that's the best way to get across with people. If you respect them and they respect you back . . .

Alissa valued respect, but also realized the importance of some interaction in the classroom.

> I don't think anybody has a right to disrespect anybody, especially, you're supposed to be here for one reason, and that's to learn. You know, socializing and just that extra stuff, seeing your friends. . . . I mean that's an extra. And it's not expected to be all strict, where you know, I don't think it should be that strict, where you have to sit in the class the whole time, not get out of your seat, just sit there and stare. You know, I think interaction with the class is good, but I don't think it should be done disrespectfully, to where they're ignoring the teacher, to where their voices are just louder than hers, or they're not listening. . . . I wouldn't have it. I would be putting a lot of people out of my class. If I was a teacher, I wouldn't put up with that, cuz there's no excuse for that. You know, I'm here to help you out. If I'm the teacher, you know, I'm doing my best. And you're gonna sit there and talk out of turn, and throw stuff across the class, and cussing and all that stuff. That's . . . in the presence of an adult, just because they are an adult, I think that much respect is due, just for the fact that they're adults. And then, if you have, if you're a good teacher, I don't know, I just don't, that's not right, definitely, for you to disrespect. But, I think, talking, should be, there should be more leniency, but, you know, within boundaries, not just to say they'd be all unruly, and screaming across the class, but I don't think it should be so strict where you have to, where you don't get to talk at all.

Johnny looks for more respect from teachers, who are, "like the juries, the teachers don't believe you and you just get in trouble. And the teachers need to believe you . . ." He explained that students sometimes have a different viewpoint, which leads to a different version of events, but the teachers call that lying and stop listening. Don concluded, "You gotta understand each other, you gotta talk a way that everybody understands."

What's a Teacher to Do?

Lewis (2001) claims that teachers tend to give students what they "deserve." They seem to prefer to punish students who act out, rather than providing them with academic help.

Respectful communication was a concern for students, who felt they could not get a hearing from some teachers or administrators and that their parents were treated discourteously.[1] We know that young people often ignore what is said and model their behavior on what they observe. Communication is an *exchange* of information or ideas. Therefore, it seems sensible that, both to get students' attention and to teach them good behavior, teachers should actively model respectful communication. This means that no matter how outrageous a student's story is, or no matter how many times we've heard it before, we need to listen carefully and respectfully. We don't have to agree or approve, just hear.[2] It also means that in addition to telling parents about our program, our rules, our goals and assignments, we need to listen to their educational beliefs.

It's hard to respect others without respecting and valuing oneself. Good teaching is a thirty-six hours-a-day job. As discussed at the beginning of the text, there is not enough time to do everything, so teachers have to set priorities, which should include time to sleep, to socialize, and to exercise. Although not directly related to the classroom, these activities help teachers immeasurably in self-control, problem solving, and achieving best practice as often as possible. A school culture in which collegial interactions are supportive rather than punitive will also reduce stress (Lewis, 2001).

Sometime during the year, the learning population can grow from a rule-based, structured environment that is monitored and controlled by the teacher to a smoothly functioning group of colleagues, working together to learn. How can the teacher facilitate that change? With the easy groups, it's a simple matter of stepping back and allowing the students to apply the social skills they've learned in the past. There are always a few individuals who need more structure, but that can be provided through individual contracts and plans. Too often, however, it's the students with good social skills who are in the minority. They can become leaders, facilitators, and peer managers as the group moves toward a more cohesive development.

As you remove structure, you must help the students replace it with a way to work together. Rules can be replaced with standards of behavior. It is difficult to state abstract values of behavior clearly enough for some students to understand them, so discussion, role playing, modeling, and stories of good examples are important in setting standards.

---

[1] *Voices from the Inside* (Poplin & Weeres, 1992) reports that parents, students, and teachers felt a lack of respect in schools.

[2] Reflective listening and active listening are two counseling techniques that have helped me learn to listen and to teach students how to listen in a communicative way.

Like the students, Meredith Minear, an experienced teacher, focuses on respect as an important standard of behavior in her class. To help develop a group understanding, she asks each student to create a small poster with the word "Respect" in large letters and clarifying terms in smaller print, pictures, and symbols. Students then place their posters about the classroom wherever they wish. It's impossible to look anywhere in the room without seeing at least one. When necessary, students' attention can be directed to a specific poster of respectful behavior and asked to consider classroom events.

Changing the Structure of the School

Schools are beginning to change their structure and programs to meet the needs of their students. An effective high school in today's world needs to base the education process on different assumptions than have traditionally guided academic practices. Exemplary programs develop from the needs of the school and the community, so each is unique.

Curriculum and delivery should shift to a more learner-centered, developmental approach. Teachers need to be compassionate and passionate, flexible, respectful, protecting, and nurturing; methods should include variety, experiences, attainable challenges, different learning and intelligence styles, highest standards, risk-taking, and an understanding of knowledge as a process rather than a state of being (Williams-Boyd, Skaggs, & Ayres, 2000).

Reilly (2000) suggests some general guidelines for learner-centered high schools:

Diverse learners' distinct perspectives must be respected and included.

Unique and changing differences of learners must be accounted for.

Relevance, engagement, and connection to prior learning enhance current learning.

Environment should be positive and interactive; the learner should be valued and supported.

Learning is natural; students' curiosity and interests should be utilized in instruction.

The teacher's job is to assist the learner.

Assessment is continuous, based on process and product.

Parental involvement is essential.

Lickona (1997) suggests students and teachers avoid guilt/punishment reactions and, instead, discuss the behavior. The teacher can offer parallel situations to clarify the concerns and help the student understand the effect of undesirable behaviors on others in the world.

Integrating curriculum is an effective teaching strategy that is an intrinsic part of many middle school programs. Some high schools are trying to increase content area connections, with varying levels of success. Pate, Homestead, and McGinnis (1997) list the components of a coherent integrated curriculum as clear goals, democratic classrooms, careful assessments, content integration, alternative pedagogies, communication within the learning community, supportive institutional structures, and reflective practice.

Democratic classrooms[3] help at-risk students, their classmates, and their teachers improve social skills (Trzyna & Miller, 1997). They lead to a decrease in youth demonization (Hyman & Snook, 2000) and in discipline problems, according to Zane (1994). Urban charter schools are primarily concerned with discipline and control at the beginning of the restructuring process. The emphasis is on disciplinary codes and clear expectations; student attitudes, their sense of responsibility, and their abilities are downgraded. As the institutions move toward

> smaller learning communities . . . shared education visions and intimate connections, . . . isolation is replaced by affiliation, antagonism by cooperation and interdependence, and impotence by risk taking. Not only does students' behavior change, but teachers' and administrators' perceptions and experiences of what constitute disciplinary problems and appropriate institutional responses shift. (pp. 122–123)

As the focus shifted from an institution of learning to a learning community, relationships improved. Democratic procedures changed the tone of faculty discussions. Relationships exchanged fragmentation in programs and hierarchies for a sense of accountability and connection, both in student behavior and teacher advocacy.

By the second year, according to Zane, student self-esteem had risen with teacher standards and support. Without tracking, the "dummies" disappeared. Teachers and students worked together to learn; they held high expectations of each other and explicitly noticed good work. As teachers showed they really cared about students' ideas, students' attitudes toward learning changed. Attendance ceased to be an issue; because they wanted to protect the program, students came prepared to work. The atmosphere was respectful rather than passive.

Zane admits these programs have drawbacks. They need a small number of students and a stable faculty to develop a strong, respectful learning environment. They do not succeed without a shared vision throughout the school. There may be difficulties integrating transfer students.

Schoenlein (2001) addresses the possibilities within larger high schools using separate buildings or the "family" or "team" concept. Fairmont High School, with 2500 students, developed a program that, over a four-year period, decreased drop-

---

[3]Pervil (1998) has an extensive resource list of information about democratic classrooms. Thomases (1998) offers activities and describes the teacher's role as facilitator. Beyer (1996) looks at the realities of building democratic practices in public school classrooms.

outs from 32 percent to 13 percent and suspensions by 25 percent. They credit specific procedures for these improvements:

> Advisories instead of home rooms, which included interadvisory games and contests, picture boards, class scheduling, parental conferences, and career planning. Advisors gave out diplomas at graduation.
>
> A semester of career planning in the sophomore year, during which all choices are honored.
>
> The enforcement of civil behavior with a "severe response" to intimidation, harassment; peer mediation; constantly available adults for counseling or action.
>
> All activities are videotaped to encourage participation.
>
> Teachers are caring and friendly.
>
> The principal models and leads the process.

Alissa gave a clear idea of what she would like as she completed her metaphor of the school as a city:

> [The community needs to] be more interactive with the government, just like how it is in the real world. I think that a lot of the time, the government has too much power, and the community doesn't have enough sayso. Or you know, when we're talking, it's just like we're talking to hear ourselves talk, there's not nobody listening. But, I mean, it could be a good city. Because I know there's a lot of people here with potential you know, that they don't even know they have. But it takes the teachers and the people in the office to bring it out of them. Because if you don't know it's there, but somebody can recognize that in you, they know what activities and assignments to give you to bring it out of you, you know, to make you a better person, that should be the focus, to keep the city going, to make it a place where somebody else might hear about it and say, "You know, that's a good place to be." You know, we come here and meet somebody, because everything is a cycle. You can't, I don't think anything is a coincidence. And say, well cuz I move a lot, I just ended up here. Well, something good will come out of it cuz you're there for a reason. Like a big city that will help.[4]

---

[4]See Forrest Gathercoal, Tom Wilson, and other proponents of democratic-style classes for ideas of a governmental approach to discipline.

9

Imagining a Creative Curriculum

Students and researchers consistently claim that the current curricula do not meet the needs of modern adolescents. As community develops in the classroom, the environment changes. Teachers become managers and facilitators rather than conduits for information. As students develop their own interests, the need for resources increases in depth and breadth. At times, learning will be at a deeper level, as students explore individual passions. As the constraints of textbooks are removed, some learners will range throughout the discipline and beyond, connecting facts and concepts to develop new understandings.

In pursuit of answers, learners may want to leave the classroom, and even the school building. Flexible scheduling may be necessary to utilize community resources.

Once we actually begin to hear students and caregivers, we can move forward in designing that "fun" education, including a program to help find the students' best fit in the world. Many of the students' ideas to improve schools and avert behavior problems could be at least partially implemented in the classroom.[1]

Teachers as advisors could help students navigate the institutional system to legislate for change and support realistic plans at faculty meetings and through their professional organizations. Changing school hours, for example, might require extensive planning, but might also increase attendance and, according to recent research on adolescent sleep patterns, should increase attention. It would solve Rebecca's immediate problem without putting her family responsibilities in conflict with her educational needs.

The school lunch program would lend itself to a great action research project for Health or Economics.[2] Students would learn why lunches are constructed the

---

[1]Each issue of *Educational Leadership* features a current educational question. There are often several articles clearly explaining specific programs being used by public schools to institute effective change. For example, a Baltimore high school has created alternative hours, returned discipline to teacher responsibility, and experienced significant decreases in typical inner city school problems.

[2]Action research is a problem-solving technique used by critical pedagogues.

way they are and perhaps come up with ideas for change. Once they have a real understanding of and voice in menu planning, leaving campus for lunch might not be an issue.

Current pedagogical theory suggests that cooperative learning enhances communication skills as well as improving content acquisition. Careful construction of cooperative learning opportunities can give students practice in effective interpersonal skills and give the teacher time to develop more personal relationships with students.

Most importantly for teachers, throughout our conversations, I heard a continual challenge to improve teaching practice. Fun was defined not as Monopoly and popular videos, but as challenge and growth. New information and skills, presented clearly and in an interesting manner, were sought and valued by the students.

Engagement in learning requires a different, fluid definition of an orderly classroom. It may lead to honest behavioral mistakes, but it also meets students' needs for fun and growth and reduces opportunities for serious problems to develop. Teachers, administrators, and parents need to understand that student-controlled learning will be messy and unpredictable. Traditional school liability roles may have to change.

Recently, I had the opportunity to see the presentations of one such class. It was made up of college seniors, so one may assume that the initial problems and student difficulties were not the same as what we see in high school. Additionally, it was an elective, so all of the students had chosen to be there.

The class was about collecting and analyzing oral histories, with a required action component. The students identified personal interests, from talking with family elders to exploring spiritual, economic, or developmental interests. The presentations were *wonderful.* I felt my mind and heart swell with a warm glow as I watched classmates raptly engrossed in their peers' comments. The stories engendered tears and laughter from audience and speaker alike. Connections were made to traditional disciplines and knowledge bases as the histories of workers were contrasted with the versions found in texts and other resources; as the histories and old age of nuns was contrasted with life and old age in the secular world; as the story of a "poor" woman with a valued family of husband and nine children was contrasted with the expectations and understandings of young undergraduates. The experience had clearly resulted in deep personal changes that would affect lives and learning experiences long after graduation. *This,* I thought, is what education is about. This is learning, growing, sharing, and thinking!

Then my "real" voice spoke up, an icicle of logic cutting through the warmth I felt. What have they learned of the canon? There are no facts and figures here, no information that we can generalize to create theory, nothing to take to graduate school, or business, or policymaking. This is all very nice, but is it worth a semester of hard work? What good is it? How will it help the students affect the world?

Results

What would happen if your class were completely student-centered, if you used your maturity and expertise to help learners develop social skills and develop their skills in your content area?

We know that an attachment to the school community and a successful academic experience will help protect schools against adolescent violence and that developmentally appropriate, active participation in education leads to increased school bonding and development of skills (Hawkins et al., 1998).

I didn't manage to create a consistently student-centered learning environment all of the time, but from the bits and pieces I've seen it's an exciting, unpredictable place to learn.[1] The classroom might be empty at times, as students leave to explore resources in the library and in the community. When there are students present, they may be quietly engrossed in an activity, conferring with the teacher, or having lively conversations among themselves, possibly about the learning at hand. Active teaching is done by student experts, the teacher, the Internet, a guest, a video, or someone's pet boa constrictor.

Cross-cultural problems become multiple assets as everyone respects and learns from different points of view (Charles, 1993; Suleiman, 2000). Resistance to learning ceases to be an issue as students design their own projects. Rebellion is focused through action research. Antisocial behavior is eroded with the need for shared expertise. Students and teacher help each other muddle through the vicissitudes of life. The special needs of all learners are addressed as individual activities develop.

At the end of the year, students leave with a continuing interest in many facets of the subject and with skills to continue their development. Action researchers can locate information and use it to change the community when necessary.

Well, it probably won't be perfect. Problems will arise, some of them as unpredictable as the directions the students will take. What I don't see in this rosy future is a Columbine, because attention to respect will make bullying and killing obsolete. What I don't see is drive-by shootings, because gangs will be too busy with action research to change their communities through violence. What I don't see is students dropping out of school because it interferes with family values, because the school will be flexible enough to meet their needs. What I don't see is students turning off because the curriculum is irrelevant, because they will be designing their own programs.

I think back to the student oral history presentations I saw and picture those learners graduating and going on in the world. Perhaps there was value to the class. As teachers and academics, these students will reframe the canon and change definitions of learning. The business majors will refocus discussions on the employee, consumer, and community member instead of limiting concerns to fiscal profit and loss. Citizens will investigate the details of statistics and government

---

[1]See Richard B. Kent's work for descriptions of a writing workshop English program that was sensitive to student needs.

decisions before making voting decisions. Students from classes like this are really going to rock the boat! Is this a good thing?

Every school needs to develop its own plan to improve the teaching/learning community. An important step is the establishment of a leadership team that includes representatives from all components of the school community: parents and students, employers and taxpayers, teachers and administrators, and both professional and paraprofessional support staff (Leone, Mayer, Mamgren, & Meisel, 2000). The biggest problem in teaching to student needs is the educational system itself. Teachers and administrators must decide if they are operating a sorting system, shunting some students into the college track, some into the vocational program, and some into dead-ends, or if they are operating a system that increases options for all students, leaving them prepared to choose their own post-secondary lives from a wide range of opportunities. Schools must work with communities who need good employees, parents who want beautiful handwriting, and a world that changes the rules for living at an increasing rate. In many cases legislative decisions must be addressed, and hard decisions about funding must be made. Above all, adults must work respectfully with young people who are confused about the changes in their bodies, minds, and roles in life, to help them build a fulfilling future, with the clear understanding this may be very different from the goals we have for them.

Some Activities to Try

By now, some students are comfortable with a student-centered learning experience and are designing their own activities. Others realize they have waited in vain for teacher guidance/requirements and are frantically searching for ways to improve their grades.

Classroom Map: As homework, ask each student to create a classroom map of what a perfect classroom would look like. The map should include room for students, a teacher, and supplies. It should convey a sense of the environment and mood the preservice teacher wants to attain. A separate sheet may be attached with a key, but only single words may be used. This is to be considered a nonverbal assignment. Content area students could map a scene from a book, a historical event, or visualize another experience.

Museum Tour: Half of the class sits with their maps, ready to discuss them with the other half, which walks around the room, looking at the plans. After five or ten minutes, reverse the groups. (This can also be used with the folder assignment, posters, or other visualizations.)

Homework: In content area groups, create a list of generic homework assignments that can be done as makeup work, when the student left materials at school, when the parent wants to see the child doing schoolwork, and so on. The list might include such tasks as current event summaries, journals, or ongoing record keeping. This can also be used with high school students who are planning their own learning.

P.O.V. Chart: In mixed groups, create a vertical list of at least five demographic variables you might expect in your classes. Consider gender, race, age , sexuality, ability, class, location, and others. In a horizontal list, put at least four ways you could observe opposite qualities or behaviors. Watch a tape of a popular television program or review the programs in a daily television listing. Tally what you observe. Compare with other group members. Discuss the results. Compare with other groups and whole class.

	Work/Play	*Happy/Sad*	*Central/Background*
Gender			
Male	'''' '' / '''	''' / '''	'''' / '''
Female	''''''' / ''''	''''''' /	'''''''' / '''''
Age			
Child			
Adolescent			
Adult			
Senior			

As homework, review a text you might use as a teacher. Whose points of view are represented? How do you know? High school students really love doing this with most texts, but be prepared for some lively critiques.

Debriefing: As a class, discuss the different types of learning you experience individually and in groups. Do people have different reactions and preferences? What is the effect of each method on learning? On behavior? This is a useful midyear discussion at the high school level. It helps both teachers and students refocus their efforts.

Volatile Issues: Show a provocative video ("The Color of Fear" and "Clockwork Orange" are both useful for instigating disagreement in education classes). Halfway through

> *Think, Pair, Share:* After a one- or two-minute quick write, each student shares ideas with a partner, then writes again.
>
> *Guided Meditation:* At the end of the video, have the students do another quick write. Lead them through a guided meditation or play soothing music while they remain still for three to five minutes. Have them write again.
>
> *Debrief:* Discuss reactions to both the video and the activities. How did they affect feelings and opinions?

Teaching Opportunities: Now is a good time for students to lead examinations of some counseling techniques, active listening, conflict resolution programs, advisory programs, and other humanistic and developmental theories. Besides being important in changing student behavior, how might they be useful in resolving teacher/student conflicts? Other conflicts within the school community? In high schools, an open calendar might help students find appropriate times to share their learning.

Building Consensus: Ask students to take sides on an issue from *Education Law* or relating to your content area. Pair individuals or small groups with a judge for six-minute debates. Have the students change sides and debate the issue again. Ask the students to create a resolution on the issue that they can all comfortably agree with. Report back to the whole group.

Brainstorming: Give a different graphic organizer to each small group. Ask groups to brainstorm solutions to school management issues or public issues in your content area, put them on graphic organizers, and report back to the group. Besides discussing ideas for change, consider the effect of the organization format on the group product.

Planning Lessons: Plan three to five lessons in your content area that would be evaluated as "fun" by the CHS teens. Test the plans with a classmate who hates the subject. Share the plans with the whole group. Ask your high school students to plan a lesson on a "boring" section or chapter.

Multiple Intelligences: In small groups, students create a poster about classroom management or a content area topic at the unit level. Using any of Gardner's identified intelligences, except verbal, present the plan to the class.

Part V

Reflections

reflections

Whenever your brain stops whirling, and at the end of the school year, it is useful to stop and think about what happened. What went well? How can you cause more of that next time? What could be improved? How can you change the classroom to increase learning? What did the students learn academically? Socially? How can you move closer to your teaching goals next year?

Summer "vacation" is also a good time to refocus and expose yourself to new ideas. Most states include continuing education requirements in their certification procedures, but informal research is also useful. On rainy days, or when it's just too hot to move, try to visit your local university library to skim through last year's professional journals. It's a good way to begin to think about different ways of doing things, to catch up on what's happening in education outside of your school, and to locate new resources for teaching content.

10

The Students' Reflections

They need to do something about when kids do something wrong; like, not sus-pending them, not giving them detention or ABC. They should do something else, try to come out with something different.

—Carla

When I started this project, my plan was to neatly lay out a hierarchy of behaviors and consequences. I tried to guide the conversations in that direction, but students always wandered back to learning and community. When I told her she was missing the point, Tracy responded, "*I'm* not missing the point! I know what you're trying to do. . . . All you *need* to do is just stop them [students who are misbehaving], or just ask them. What you don't do is send them to ABC!" So I began to focus more on the question, "What would you do if you were running the school? How would you treat a student like you?"

Like adult educators, the students had many different, often contradictory opinions about behavior management. Punishment played a role in everybody's plan, but proactive, problem-solving approaches were even more important in their discussions. Everyone wished for increased respect among all members of the school community and believed that open communication was the key. Listening could result in constructive changes in scheduling, structure, teaching, and rules.

Punishment and Change

Time to learn his lesson.

—Johnny

Most students believed that there is a time when punishment is an appropriate consequence for continued misbehavior. Violence, substance abuse on campus, and classroom disruptions should be punished, and repeated lateness, frequent ditching, and unwarranted disrespect also deserved a negative consequence. Like other members of the education community, they disagreed about the timing and severity of punishments. They did, however, agree that consequences should not be automatic, but rather that communication should be emphasized, and, whenever possible, logical consequences should be used instead of arbitrary punishments.

Tracy was concerned with adult misbehaviors:

> Behaviors that would not be allowed? Like proctors harassing the kids, for no reason. Um, teachers just like yelling at the kids. Like, sometimes they don't bring their homework, they don't ask them why, they're just like, "Detention. You didn't bring your work." They don't want to hear why on that. Or if you didn't understand, they're like, "How come you didn't ask in class?" Cuz I understand in class, but when you got home, you forgot. And explain it better.

In order to deter future misbehavior, many students believed that punishments must be more severe than the current systems. Antashia observed, "If you're gonna punish somebody . . . you never stick to it. That's why people take advantage of punishment, or the punishment's not harsh enough." Carla, too, pointed out that rules must be consistently enforced. She suggested that an in-school suspension could be useful, if students were truly prohibited from socializing all day and if they were given appropriate assignments to work on. Don also suggested some sort of very strict alternative schooling "for like two weeks, they come back out of that school learning something," ready to behave in their classes. Chaquan insisted on alternative schooling for students who could not manage to behave. She said, "I wouldn't kick no kids out of school, cuz everybody needs their education." Nivek suggested that there should be separate places for students who want to study and those who want to talk or fool around. He said, "I don't feel comfortable about it when kids mess around and everything like that. I try to put my mind on one thing or another. . . . Without being a bother to anyone, I want to study."

Several students complained that Saturday School, although it was an effective deterrent because it disrupted their plans, was a waste of time. Chaquan wanted activities to be provided, as they did in her previous school, but also wondered if there couldn't be some sort of a makeup class for credit, so that students could catch up on work they have missed, instead of continuing to fall further behind. Stephanie thought that cleaning up the campus would be a good activity for Saturday School. Alissa agreed, explaining,

> . . . if you try to talk to them, they have that bad attitude toward, it's like, "Oh, forget you. I don't care what you say, I'm gonna do what I want, no matter what you say, da da da." I would just put them to work.

She added that she would not limit the time to Saturday, but look for the most inconvenient time for the student. She hoped:

> Something positive can come out of it too. They're negative in their class, and inconveniencing the teachers and the other people around them. Take that and do something good with it. Put them to work. Show, help the school look nicer, do something productive. . . . I think the word would get out sooner or later, cuz nobody likes to clean up, barely after your own self, but after other people. . . . I think the work would get out and they'd be like, "Man, you know, two steps away from the trash can and you just want to throw it down on the ground. Go to the trash can and put it in the trash!" The word would definitely get out. Take that extra step to the trash can, it won't kill you. And when you're done, flush the toilet, cuz I don't want to reach my hand in there and pull out nothing you put in there. You know, just basic things, that you do at home. If you're at home, you don't do that kind of stuff, so why would you come, you know, this is your home away from home. You spend a lot of time here. If you don't do it at home, because you know you don't like things, you don't like your environment to be that way: all smelly and dirty and trashy, that's embarrassing. Why would you come to another place, where other people have to be, and treat it like that? That doesn't make any sense.
>
> I would definitely put them to work and make them clean up, and I think sooner or later the word would get out to clean up after yourselves. You don't do this at home. If your mom was sitting here in front of you, you know, she wouldn't want you to do this. You wouldn't do it in front of your mom, don't do it in front of this teacher. Don't do it in front of other students. It's rude, it's inconsiderate. There's just no reason for it. I think eventually, they'll get the picture to throw your trash away. You make the mess. . . . You know, if you can't clean it up, get a janitor or somebody. Wipe up your stuff. I don't see what's the big deal. Ask for a napkin or something. You know. Just little things they can do, to make stuff better. And they don't take that, that one extra step.

There was disagreement about off-campus suspension. Some students felt it was a logical and sensible consequence. Rebecca explained, "If you want to be disruptive, you're gonna fail anyways, right? So might as well take it out from the class instead of disrupting others. . . ." If students cannot learn to behave, they should be suspended again. The resulting loss of credit is a logical punishment that may deter future misbehavior. Don would suspend fighters. Stephanie would not have Saturday School, but just suspend students until they were ready to behave.

Both Angela and Carla were against suspension, for different reasons. Angela believed suspension is "dumb, because you're just giving students a vacation. They should make them stay in school and do something. . . . [Don't] tell them, 'You guys can't come to school,' cuz they don't want to come to school anyway!" Carla saw suspension as a denial of education and an opportunity for the student to get into more trouble on the street.

Students were ambivalent about the security personnel on campus. Angela wanted more proctors, to guard every exit. Johnny thought the proctors were acceptable, but wanted to get rid of the school police, because, "they treat us like punks." He claimed they took students' property, conducted illegal searches, and hit students with their sticks. Robert, who spoke the most about illegal and dangerous activity on campus, was the most pessimistic. He said, "The only way to stop any of this, is, honestly, is the [Mexican] Mafia." He explained that the Mafia had, in the past two years, virtually eradicated tagging and the attendant violence in this town. He worried about the fact that the security police carry guns, which then become accessible to the students. He suggested that, instead of patrolling the campus and ineffectually guarding the exits, proctors stand on the roof. They can see who leaves and report them to the office. Those without excuses can be punished with ABC or suspension the next day.

Both Robert and Casper discussed the issue of guns and other contraband on campus. Both rejected the use of stationary metal detectors as being too easy to circumvent and as being more of a challenge than a deterrent. Robert suggested:

> If they would grab the kids at random, just, you know, "You, come here. I want to check you." They would catch so many things. Because if you summons a kid to the office, like me, you know, when they used to summons me to the office, I would leave my bag. I would tell them, "Hey, keep my bag. If I don't come back, just take my bag, I'll pick it up after." I might have markers in my bag, my knife, whatever. But, like, I used to carry a pager, because my mom was sick. I would tell them, "Hey take my pager. I don't want to get caught with it." I'd go to the office, by the time I got to the office, I had nothing with me, not even a pencil. They would check me, "What do you have?" "I ain't got nothing." By the time you get to the office, you know, you've already dumped everything everywhere.

Tom felt that the school should not even deal with students who broke the law, but just turn them over to the police for legal action. The police should then at least take them to the station and "lock them up for a few hours and then talk to them. So they got scared, and next time. . . ." He felt that fear is a strong deterrent and should be used in the case of endangerment, such as during the school riots.

Just Change

On the other hand, Tom thought that simple misdemeanors, such as tardiness or ditching, should be treated much more leniently than is the current practice. Students should be able to have perhaps three unexcused absences each semester before they are assigned ABC or Saturday School. Being ten or fifteen minutes late to class was also acceptable to him.

Most students agreed with Tom about lateness. They felt that first, school starts too early. The starting time should be changed. Second, students often have a legitimate reason for being late to class. Missing the material is adequate punishment for inadvertent lateness and should be a reason to avoid future tardiness. Antashia summarized all the students' feeling when she said, "If you late and you ditch, it means your grade is gonna reflect that. That means you're gonna take the class over."

Both Alissa and Antashia wanted all students to be eligible for an off-campus lunch pass, which could be withdrawn if abused. Antashia pointed out that teachers can leave campus for lunch and that many do so because the food on campus is not very good. Most students felt occasional ditching was acceptable, as long as grades didn't suffer. Tracy and Johnny would want to find out why the student is ditching. A personality conflict between teacher and student might result in a schedule change rather than punishment for the student.

Frequent complaints about a specific teacher would warrant a hidden tape recorder, so that the principal could find out what is really going on in the class and discipline the true offender, who may well be the teacher. Tracy suggested that the principal's job also include circulating through the school and ". . . like, pop up in there and see . . . what the student is talking about."

Alissa and Tom specifically mentioned changing rules about the use of bathrooms. Alissa would eliminate the privilege of senior restrooms and open them to all students. Tom would not allow teachers to forbid the students to leave class to use a restroom.

Tracy and Chaquan liked the rotating schedule in their previous school. They enjoyed the variations in routine, but also believed that they had certain "good" learning times during the day. Rotating the schedule helped them spread the good times across the curriculum and diluted the effect of the bad times on any particular class.

Johnny, Carla, and Nivek disliked the dress code and would eliminate it. At the beginning of the discussion, Nivek supported the dress code as a means of suppressing gang activity, but as he thought about it he decided:

> I didn't like that cuz I like to dress the way I want to, I feel comfortable the way I am. . . . I think they do, too, because, well, people have their own ways to feel comfortable the way they dress and their own manners and everything.

Tracy, Chaquan, and Don believed it was important to consider the individual situation more closely. Tracy would talk to a student, then design a consequence, which might be a punishment, to fit the student and the situation. Chaquan, who was very concerned that mothers were unable to check on their children during the riots, felt that there are certain times when rules must be bent to meet more important needs. Don saw a need to monitor, encourage, and pressure problem students constantly, to help those students learn appropriate behavior.

Antashia believed that the school should make some simple changes to develop a sense of community and reduce conflicts.

> Like you know, start making the school better for us. We sit here, we come to school all day. I know, in some parts, in some part of the day, or we're gonna leave school and go have fun on our own. And go get some excitement on our own. And we come to school, it's no fun, it's boring.

She explains that current school attempts to provide activities only exacerbate the problems.

> We'll have lunch dances. But at lunch dances, they play like three, four English songs; lunch is thirty minutes long, but when we have that, it's extended lunch. So it's probably like an hour. And the rest is Spanish songs. Which makes people mad, which starts a fight, cuz they be like, "Ew. Why they playing that?" Then the Mexicans, you know, "That's our kind of music."

Very offended by monies wasted on ineffectual security measures, Robert suggested developing student talents by providing specific classes and activities. Taggers, for example, are artists, who with proper guidance and materials, could decorate the school and community with murals. Athletes who could not always afford the cost of insurance and supplies for sports sometimes use their skills to evade proctors and school police in exhilarating chases on and off campus. Perhaps funding sports access for all interested students would avert the need for so much security on campus.

Students agreed that part of the problem with discipline in schools is which rules are enforced and for whom. Many suggested not only specific rule changes, but also a change in the way rules are made. Alissa believed, "Administration, and parents and students, everybody should be interacting."

Parents should be included in rule making because, as Tom said, "Students are part of their parents." Besides, he added, they pay the school taxes and have a right to be involved in rule making. Ana and Robert, as new parents, wanted to know what their child was doing. They believed that they could raise him to inform them of his actions and, as parents, they could decide whether these actions, such as ditching, were appropriate; and they could then decide what reactions would be most effective.

Although students also should be included in the rule-making process, Tom pointed out that they may be unrealistic or try to take advantage of the system. Others were aware of their current position as learners, rather than leaders, and were reluctant to make suggestions about what should be done. Angela, unsure of what to do with problem students, said, "These pressures [detention and suspension] don't work for them. . . . I don't know . . . maybe when I'm older. . . ." Stephanie realized that she had matured in the past few years, but she was not yet experienced enough to make decisions for others. Tracy, a first-year high school student, believed that older students should have stricter behavior standards than she and share in the responsibility for teaching her how to behave.

Alissa saw the rules, and learning how to circumvent them, as actually being part of her school learning experience: "We can only take what's there for us; if we find a way around it and change it and make it work for us, not necessarily hurting anybody, but, making it work for us, that's part of becoming an adult." Rebecca agreed that warnings were a form of advice that informs students about the consequences of their actions. Punishment was necessary, although not always effective:

> Because you can't get away with everything, just like that, just so easy. Cuz if he gets away with it, without nobody telling him anything, or punishing him, he'll just keep doing it. He'll go, "Well, this is ok. So nobody's going to tell me anything, so I can just do it over again." . . . For some people. . . . It doesn't work on all people.

Students realized that the school can't do everything; some students will not change, for many reasons. Although several talked about incorrigible students, they were talking about others, not themselves. Don explained, "There's gonna be somebody in the group that's gonna start something. So you can't. . . . There's bad people everywhere you look and go. . . ." They also felt that discipline may have become too important in schools. They suspected that the focus needs to change; Nivek, for example, knew that he needed to concentrate on "learning and finish(ing) school."

After considering the options, Antashia concluded, "No, it's not really about punishment . . . punishment's not always the answer. It could be other things."

Communication

> *You need somebody to talk to you, not at you.*
>
> —Tracy

Issues of communication arose throughout the discussions. Students often complained that teachers and administrators did not listen. They were also concerned about how students talked to teachers and each other. When asked what they would do as principal, all of the students responded that they would first listen to the student, then they would often contact the parent to inform or ask for help. Most students said that punishment, often in the form of ABC or Saturday School, was a reasonable consequence only *after* other alternatives had been examined.

The principal or disciplinarian has two functions: to counsel and to judge. As a counselor, the administrator should listen to understand. Tracy preferred to go to certain administrators rather than others because she knew, "They'll listen and they'll get to the bottom of it. They'll listen to what I have to say all the way through, instead of disagreeing with me or just giving me ABC or whatever." They should first explain why the behavior is unacceptable so that the student can adapt to the school. Johnny added that up to five warnings could be justified but Don disagreed:

> What they need to do is put their feet down; you do it this time, you gotta go out. First time it goes out. You don't keep giving them chances, cuz the more chances you give them, and the more and more, they just gonna do it and do it. . . . See, that's why you gotta say, "I'm putting my foot down, you gotta go out right now." First time.

Stephanie said if she were principal:

> I would tell them that teachers don't like the way they're behaving, and that when the teachers tell you what to do, you follow that. And if they still don't cooperate and keep up what they're doing, then I'll just have to, I guess, keep them in my office, until they really know how to clean up their act.

Disciplinarians should encourage students, help students find alternative ways to do things, but also, sometimes just lay down the law and, if necessary, punish.

Johnny, after listening to a student's version of a teacher-student conflict, would advise the student and either closely monitor the student's progress and grade or, if necessary, change the student to another class.

As judge, the disciplinarian needs to know all sides of the story. Tracy reminded administrators, "Don't always jump to believe the teacher, listen to the student, too, cuz they're people too." Too often, the student's side is ignored, so problems, although they may be covered up, are not solved. Don said, "Actually, you gotta listen to both of the sides. If you just take the teacher's side all the time, the student may be right and the teacher would be wrong at times." The punishment may stop the student from acting out, but poor teaching continues. As in the court system, judges also should consider past behavior and reason for breaking a rule. When discussing lateness, Alissa said:

> I don't think it's reasonable. I think each, each case, I mean it might take, be time consuming, but I think each case should be looked at, because say, you're a straight A student and you have, either you live far away or, you know, you have car trouble, or if you have to depend on somebody else for a ride, or every once in a while you're sick and you're having a slow morning, and if you take just little mistakes that can happen, little, little, you know, things could pop up and make you late. Say if you're only one minute late, or you get right to the door and the bell rings before you're in your seat, you know, stuff like that. I don't think, I don't think that's fair. I think they should look at everybody's circumstances before they just say, "Oh, you know . . ." And then, if you were tardy since they made up the policy, there's, what, six months left of school? If you were tardy once a month, I mean, you know, things are gonna happen to where you're late. And if you're tardy once a month, you get dropped from that class. I think that's kind of harsh. I mean, just to say that for everybody. I

could see, if they saw people who were purposely ditching, and purposely coming in late cuz they didn't care, then I think they should look at everybody's circumstances. And see what, you know, don't just say, "OK, you're tardy," and you know they have to go through detention and ABC and all that stuff. If they have a good reason, or if it was out of their hands as to why they were late, I don't think they should be punished for it.

I think I'd go into details on everything. I'd look at that person's record, to see if their attendance is up, and how their citizenship is, does this person really care, or are they just doing it to be rebellious? What? I mean I'd look at it like that. And set it up that way. I couldn't, because since I know how it is, I just couldn't punish everybody. Just, you know, just couldn't do it. I don't know why. Cuz you know, some people . . . live far away. And it'll like take an hour, forty-five minutes, and a lot of people don't like to walk. But they're depending on their parents, by riding in their parents, you know, they're having a slow morning, they have to go to work, whatever. They have other people in the house to get ready for school and stuff like that. You have to wait for them and they're driving up and you're getting out of the car and you hear the tardy bell and you're like, "I'm stuck!" So, you know, it seems like that happens. I would just have to look at each and every circumstance before I applied that rule. That I wouldn't just say, "Everybody," that I would listen first.

Angela also wanted to get to the root of the problem. For example, fighting is a situation that is rarely alleviated by punishing the participants.

I think, I don't know. I guess they need to talk to whoever they're having problems with, they're supposed to see what's going on, because if you sent somebody to detention, that didn't solve anything, because whenever they meet again, they'll just bring it back up, they'll start it all over again. So I don't think detention is helping fighting, if people get in fights, they need to get the two people who are in the fight and sit down and talk to them to see what's going on.

Don would talk to all participants in a fight to try to solve the problem, but he would suspend both students, because he does not want fighting on his campus. (Other students agreed that all fighters had to be talked to, but felt that only the instigators should be punished.) Casper believed he was helped whenever he had a clear contract between him and school.

Many problems could be avoided if the teacher would listen to the student. Don gave one example:

Teachers have to understand kids, too. You know, kids have problems; teachers have problems, you know. Well, most, many of the kids have problems because teachers don't want to listen to what the kids is saying. Like if I say, "Oh, Mr. Forrest, this kid right here did such and such to me, and they won't listen to you. . . . Well, Mr. Forrest, he'll listen, that's one thing about him, he will listen. Well, most teachers be like, "Oh, yeah, whatever, go sit down." You know. And they'll just say, "Well, the next time you do it, I'm gonna send you out."

Stephanie related how Mr. Green will say, "'Get your work done!' I go, 'My work's already done.' And then he'll let me kick back and do what I want." Chaquan said her behavior changes when teachers "let *me* talk, and then maybe. . . ." However, she rarely had an opportunity to present her side of a story to a teacher. Tracy explained that "some reasons why kids cause problems is cuz you don't want to listen to them." When a teacher cursed at her, she wanted to "cuss right back at them!" but could not under the present system of discipline. She expected the teacher, as an adult, to have more patience, but instead, the younger, less experienced person had to exercise control.

The students agreed that parent involvement could be an essential factor in school-student interactions. Alissa explained:

> I think it's important for parent involvement, whether you have to call the house, or you know, invite them to the school. . . . I think if something . . . was going on, you have to start talking to the parents, or whoever is in charge of them, before they leave. . . . I just really think it should be as much as you can do to help the student. . . . I think it should be more parent involvement. Administration and parents and students everybody should be interacting.

Many students believed even the threat of parent involvement to be an effective deterrent. When discussing ditching, Carla said,

> I would just call their parents. And then you would get in trouble for that. Cuz like my friends are like, "Uh uhh, they're gonna call my parents, I'm not gonna go." And they go, "Nah, nah, they're not, they're not." And then they do, and they won't ditch any more, cuz their parents . . .

Chaquan added:

> Some kids probably stay home and get the mail first. They need to try and get in touch with all the parents. . . . They [the parents] need to find out what's going on.
> But some parents don't really care. There's a lot of kids up here, they come to school when they want to, and they leave and whatever, and their parents don't care. . . . I don't think there is nothing to do. . . . If they don't care, then there's nothing I can do.

She concluded that parents may superficially seem not to care, but that they don't always understand how serious their child's problem is. If they were informed, most parents would become involved. Tom would consult parents immediately, to see how they want to deal with the situation. He would be very courteous to the parents, something he has not seen in his current interactions with the disciplinarian. After listening to the parents, he would talk to the student.

Students had a clear picture of the continuum of the disciplinarian's responsibilities. They would talk to the student, look at the student's reasons, and design a plan for change, which often included the teacher. If behavior did not improve, they would then bring in the parents for support, and finally assign a detention or suspension. Even then, Johnny would work with the student to find a good time for the punishment. Tracy, however, was firm in her conviction that students' problems need to be solved in school, through discussion, not punishment. She says, "Seems like some kids, they just wanna have fun." But punishment doesn't change these behaviors either, so she would just continue to work with these students until they were ready for change.

Chaquan added that administrators also need to listen to students about schoolwide problems. She said that when students tried to discuss the riot with the principal, his response was,

> "I do not care about that right now. You guys need to be part of the problem or the solution." That's what got a lot of the kids mad, that he didn't care. . . . He wanted us to get it together. He wasn't even around. He went back to his office. He didn't know about anything.

11

The Reflective Teacher

Besides a lot of effort and creativity, an interactive disciplinary approach requires a lot of thought. Teachers need to think quickly, reacting appropriately to a myriad of classroom situations. We also need to think slowly, reflecting upon previous classes and laying a foundation for quick thinking in future situations.

When students came to me with legitimate complaints about school and teachers, I often said, "You can't change anyone but yourself," and talked with them about how to fit in with a teacher's requirements. I still think that's a good survival skill, but I'm pretty sure it's a bad answer.

Today I would do more work with problem-solving skills as part of the curriculum. We might role-play Lady Macbeth, Macbeth, and Banquo, using a conflict resolution technique; or work with enslavers and the enslaved to reach a consensual arrangement; or actively listen to at least five explanations of the beginning of our world. Additionally, I would challenge myself and other teachers to use these processes in resolving our differences with students, not as a tool to manipulate compliance, but as a means of personal growth for the participants and mutually sensible changes for the institution.

We're on our own in the classroom, but reflection can be useful with students and colleagues as well as individually. Students sometimes enjoy debriefing an experience such as the riots at CHS. They can consider its effect on themselves and others, develop and role play alternative scenarios, or express themselves with creative projects. Colleagues are an invaluable source of support, information, and ideas. A good carpool partner can be a life saver! Solitary reflection helps sort out feelings, intuitions, and priorities. It is important to remember, whether together or alone, to spend more time reflecting on how to increase the good stuff than on how to avoid more problems. It is also wise to try to deal with negatives at the beginning of the class or week and to celebrate the positives as you leave.

Although the students contradicted each other and themselves, they seemed to be in agreement on some central issues. They did not usually question the need for punishment, but were concerned with the mechanical way in which it is assigned. They thought communication with the student should be an initial and ongoing response to a behavior problem. The students believed that their role in life

Some Questions for Reflection

1. What are your goals?

2. How do you define "effective"?

3. What has worked or failed in the past?

4. What kind of class do your students want?

5. What are your resources?

at this time is to learn, and they did learn from the school's discipline system. Unfortunately, they learned evasive skills rather than obedience to rules. Those who seemed to be more successful at fitting into the system had relinquished their idea of school as an educational opportunity and readjusted their goals to amass course credits and achieve grades. Most felt that the discipline system demonstrated a lack of respect for their needs and their humanity. Is this an acceptable system? How do teachers affect it?

Students are looking for help as they learn how to fit into the real world. They are willing to take responsibility for their actions, but want help with their mistakes and false starts rather than punishment for them. The questions faced by more and more teachers are: What is the students' reality? How is it best to function there? When is escape a better plan? Who decides? What is a teacher's role? A parent's? A student's?

Kids are both more resilient and more fragile than I expected. Wisely, most use their strength to protect themselves from harmful schooling. When ready, they trust some teachers to assist them in growing up. I wish we could address their strengths, rather than battle them; respect their goals, even though they may conflict with our vision of a good life; and, above all, honor their potentials by providing them with safe, challenging growth opportunities. I think as we approach these goals, schooling will become education, and disciplinary challenges will become opportunities for all of us to learn. Isn't that the business of schools?

Teachers can work for change in the schools and increased communication in the classroom without decreasing subject matter acquisition, although the content covered may change. We can use current research, professional literature, collegial expertise, student perceptions, and our own creativity to develop classroom programs that encourage mutually desirable behaviors.

Bibliography and References

Abi-Nader, J. (1990). "A house for my mother": Motivating Hispanic students. *Anthropology and Education Quarterly, 21* (1), 41–58.

Adams, S. (1986). Saturday Work Adjustment Program for school discipline. *Education, 106* (3), 335–337.

Adelman, H. S. (1989). Toward solving the problems of misidentification and limited intervention efficacy. *Journal of Learning Disabilities, 22* (10), 608–612.

Adelman, H. S., & Taylor L. (1983). Enhancing motivation for overcoming learning and behavior problems. *Journal of Learning Disabilities, 16* (7), 384–392.

Agran, M. (1997). *Student directed learning: Teaching self-determination skills.* Pacific Grove, CA: Brooks/Cole.

Alberto, P. A., & Troutman, A. C. (1999). *Applied behavior analysis for teachers.* Upper Saddle River, NJ: Merrill.

Alpert, B. (1991). Students' resistance in the classroom. *Anthropology and Education Quarterly, 22* (4), 350–366.

Anderson, T. (1998). Democratic classrooms: Addressing the needs of children at risk. *Primary Voices—K–6, 7* (2), 13–19.

Armstrong, C. (1992). The control myth: Why you're still getting sassed by kids. *Vocational Education Journal, 67* (7), 34, 78.

Arnold, J. (1984). Values of exceptional students during early adolescence. *Exceptional Children, 51* (3), 230–234.

Bacon, C. S. (1993). Student responsibility for learning. *Adolescence, 28* (109), 199–211.

Barclay, W. (1959). *Train up a child.* Philadelphia: The Westminster Press.

Barritt, L., Beekman, T., Bleeker, H., & Mulderij, K. (1985). *Researching educational practice.* University of North Dakota: Center for Teaching and Learning.

Bartlett, L. (1989). Disciplining handicapped students: Legal issues in light of *Honig v. Doe. Exceptional Children, 55* (4), 357–366.

Belenkey, M. F., Clinchy, B. M., Goldberger, N. R., & Tarule, J. M. (1997). *Women's ways of knowing: The development of self, voice, and mind.* New York: BasicBooks.

Bell, R. H. (1988). An investigation of the effectiveness of a Saturday School program in reducing the rate of truancy among ninth and tenth grade habitually tardy students (Doctoral dissertation, University of the Pacific, 1988). *Dissertation Abstracts International, 49,* AAC8819497.

Bender, W. N., & Smith, J. K. (1990). Classroom behavior of children with learning disabilities: A meta-analysis. *Journal of Learning Disablities, 23* (5), 298–305.

Beyer, L. E. (Ed.). (1996). *Creating democratic classrooms: The struggle to integrate theory and practice.* New York: Teacher's College Press.

Blaetter, R. B. (1991). An analysis of alternative-to-suspension programs and their effectiveness in California public high schools (Doctoral dissertation, University of La Verne, 1991). *Dissertation Abstracts International, 52,* AAC9212106.

Black, K. A. (2000). Gender differences in adolescents' behavior during conflict resolution talks with best friends. *Adolescence, 35* (139), 499–512.

Blair, H. (1994). Voice for indigenous youth: Literature for adolescents. In S. Steffey & W. J. Hood (Eds.), *If this is social studies, Why isn't it boring?* York, ME: Stenhouse Publishers.

Block, J. (1987, April). *Longitudinal antecedents of ego-control and ego-resiliency in late adolescence.* Paper presented at the Biennial Meeting of the Society for Research in Child Development, Baltimore MD.

Borman, K. M. (1988). Playing on the job in adolescent work settings. *Anthropology and Education Quarterly, 19* (2), 163–181.

Boscardin, M. L. (1987). Local level special education due process hearings: Cost issues surrounding individual student differences. *Journal of Education Finance, 12* (3), 391–402.

Brown, W. E., & Payne, T. (1988). Policies/practices in public school discipline. *Academic Therapy, 23* (3), 297–301.

Brubaker, J. S. (1947). *A history of the problems of education.* New York: McGraw-Hill.

Bowen, G. L., Bowen, N.K., & Richman, J. M. (2000). School size and middle school students' perceptions of the school environment. *Social Work in Education, 22* (2), 69–82.

Butchart, R. E., & McEwan, B. M. (Eds.). (1998). *Classroom discipline in American schools: Problems and possibilities for democratic education.* Albany: State University of New York Press.

Butts, R. F. (1947). *A cultural history of education.* New York: McGraw-Hill.

Butts, R. F. (1955). *A cultural history of Western education: Its social and intellectual foundations.* New York: McGraw-Hill.

Butts, R. F. (1973). *The education of the West: A formative chapter in the history of civilization.* New York: McGraw-Hill.

Bybee, R. W., & Gee, E. G. (1982). *Violence, values and justice in the schools.* Boston: Allyn and Bacon.

Calhoun, M. L., & Beattie, J. (1987). School competence needs of mildly handicapped adolescents. *Adolescence, 22* (87), 555–563.

Campbell, D. W. (1991). A case study of discipline problems in an urban middle school (Doctoral dissertation, Temple University, 1991). *Dissertation Abstracts International, 52,* AAC9120783.

Carter, R. S., & Wojtkiewicz, R. A. (2000). Parental involvement with adolescents' education: Do daughters or sons get more help? *Adolescence, 35* (137), 29–44.

Charles, J. (1993). *The democracy of inclusion: American Indian literatures in the English Language Arts classroom.* Paper presented at the Annual Meeting of the National Council of Teachers of English (Pittsburgh, PA, November 17–22).

Chizak, L. (1984). We use a detention room to keep kids' behavior problems in check. *American School Board Journal, 171* (7), 29–30.

Cleary, L. M., & Peacock, T. D. (1998). *Collected wisdom: American Indian education.* Boston: Allyn and Bacon.

Cohen, M. W. (1986). Intrinsic motivation in the special education classroom. *Journal of Learning Disabilities, 19* (5), 258–261.

Collard, M. (2001). *The golden teacher.* Unpublished paper.

Collins, J. (1988). Language and class in minority education. *Anthropology and Education Quarterly, 19* (4), 299–326.

Conover, P. J. (1988, April). *Detention as a deterrent for late assignments: A study.* Paper presented at the Annual Meeting of the American Educational Research Association, Boston, MA.

Cornwall, A., & Bowden, H. N. (1992). Reading disabilities and agression: A critical review. *Journal of Learning Disabilities, 25* (5), 281–288.

Council for Exceptional Children. (1998). *What every special educator must know*. Reston, VA: Author.

Coyle, M. (1989). Vocational education and the at-risk student. *TASSP Brief*. Berkeley, CA: Technical Assistance for Special Populations Program.

Crews, G. A., & Counts, M. R. (1997). *The evolution of school disturbance in America: Colonial times to modern day*. Westport, CT: Praeger.

Cromer, J. L. (1997). *The state of our nation's youth: 1997–1998*. Alexandria, VA: Horatio Alger Association.

Darling-Smith, B. (Ed.) (1993). *Can virtue be taught?* Notre Dame: Notre Dame Press.

Deci, E. L., Hodges, R., Peirson, L., & Tomassone, J. (1992). Autonomy and competence as motivational factors in students with learning disabilities and emotional handicaps. *Journal of Learning Disabilities, 25* (7), 457–471.

Delgado-Gaitan, C. (1988). The value of conformity: Learning to stay in school. *Anthropology and Education Quarterly, 19* (4), 354–381.

Delpit, L. (1995). *Other people's children: Cultural conflict in the classroom*. New York: The New Press.

Deslandes, R., & Rayer, E. (1997). Family-related variables and school disciplinary events at the secondary level. *Behavior Disorders, 23* (1), 18–28.

DeVos, G. A., & Suárez-Orozco, M. (1990). *Status inequality: The self in culture*. Newbury Park, CA: Sage Publications.

Deyhle, D., & LeCompte, M. (1994). Cultural differences in child development: Navajo adolescents in middle schools. *Theory into Practice, 33* (3), 156–165.

Dinkins, H. K. (1981). Disciplinary problems and corrective measures in South Carolina secondary schools (Doctoral dissertation, University of South Carolina, 1981) *Dissertation Abstracts International, 42,* AAC8129452.

Dohrman, T. E. (1987). A case study of the Saturday suspension program operated by the New Hanover County Schools (Doctoral dissertation, The University of North Carolina at Chapel Hill, 1987). *Dissertation Abstracts International, 49,* AAC8821433.

Doyle, W. (1978). Are students behaving worse than they used to behave? *Journal of Research and Development in Education, 11* (4), 3–17.

Doyle, W. (1990). Classroom management techniques. In O. C. Moles (Ed.), *Student discipline strategies: Research and practice* (pp. 113–128). Albany: State University of New York Press.

Duke, D. L. (1978). Looking at the school as a rule-governed organization. *Journal of Research and Development in Education, 11* (4), 116–126.

Duncan, M. P. A. (1991). Perceptions of South Carolina public secondary school administrators toward major student discipline problems (Doctoral dissertation, University of South Carolina, 1991). *Dissertation Abstracts International, 52,* AAC9200797.

Dunham, R. G., & Alpert, G. P. (1987). Keeping juvenile delinquents in school: A prediction model. *Adolescence, 22* (85), 45–57.

Eby, F. (1952). *The development of modern education*. New York: Prentice-Hall.

Eisenman, L. T., & Chamberlin, M. (2001). Implementing self-determination activities: Lessons from schools. *Remedial and Special Education, 22* (3), 138–147.

Elam, S. M., et al. (1992). The 24th annual Gallup/Phi Delta Kappa poll of the public's attitudes toward public schools. *Phi Delta Kappan, 72* (1), 41–53.

Elkind, D. (1984). *All grown up and no place to go: Teenagers in crisis*. Reading, MA: Addison-Wesley.

Elliot, D. S., Hambert, B. A., & Williams, K. R. (1998). *Violence in American schools*. New York: Cambridge University Press.

Emblen, D. L. (1969). For a disciplinarian's manual. *Phi Delta Kappan, 50* (6), 339–340.

Erdman, R. D., & Manning, T. J. (1987, April). *PROVE Schools: The extended school day program: A study in programming, philosophy and direction*. Paper presented at the Annual convention of the Council for Exceptional Children Chicago, IL.

Erickson, F. (1987). Transformation and school success: The politics and culture of educational achievement. *Anthropology and Education Quarterly, 18* (4), 335–356.

Fagan, J., & Wilkinson, D. L. (1998). Social contexts and functions of adolescent violence. In D. S. Elliot, B.A. Hambert, & K. R. Williams. (Eds.), *Violence in American schools.* New York: Cambridge University Press.

Feldhusen, J. F. (1978). Behavior problems in secondary schools. *Journal of Research and Development in Education, 11* (4), 17–28.

Fine, M. (1991). *Framing dropouts: Notes on the politics of an urban public high school.* Albany: State University of New York Press.

Fine, M. (Ed.). (1994). *Chartering urban school reform: Reflections on public high schools in the midst of change.* New York: Teachers College Press.

Fine, M., Weis, L., & Powell, L. C. (1997). Communities of difference: A critical look at desegregated spaces created for youth. *Harvard Educational Review, 67* (2), 247–284.

Finifter, A. W. (1972). *Alienation and the social system.* New York: John Wiley & Sons.

Fordham, S. (1993). "Those loud Black girls": (Black) women, silence and gender "passing" in the academy. *Anthropology and Education Quarterly, 24* (1), 3–32.

Gaddy, G. D. (1988). High school order and academic achievement. *American Journal of Education, 96* (4), 496–518.

Galbo, J. J. (1989). The teacher as significant adult: A review of the literature. *Adolescence, 24* (95), 449–556.

Gathercoal, F. (1998). Judicious discipline. In R. Butchart & B. McEwan (Eds.), *Classroom discipline in American schools: Problems and possibilities for democratic education.* Albany: State University of New York Press.

Gibson, M. A. (1987). The school performance of immigrant minorities: A comparative view. *Anthropology and Education Quarterly, 18* (4), 262–275.

Gilligan, C. (1982). *In a different voice.* Cambridge: Harvard University Press.

Gilligan, C., Rogers, A. G., & Tolman, D. L. (Eds.). (1991). *Women, girls, and psychotherapy: Reframing resistance.* New York: The Hawthorn Press.

Gilmore, P. (1985). "Gimme room": School resistance, attitudes, and access to literacy. *Journal of Education, 167* (1), 111–128.

Glasser, W. (1985). Discipline has never been the problem and isn't the problem now. *Theory into Practice, 24* (4), 241–246.

Glasser, W. (1990). *The quality school: Managing students without coercion.* New York: Harper Perennial.

Goldstein, A. P., Harootunian, B., & Conoley, J. C. (1994). *Student aggression: Prevention, management and replacement training.* New York: The Guilford Press.

Gootman, M. E. (1998). Effective in-house suspension. *Educational Leadership, 56* (1), 39–41.

Gottfredson, D. C., Gottfredson, G. D., & Hybl, L. G. (1993). Managing adolescent behavior: A multiyear, multischool study. *American Educational Research Journal, 30* (1), 179–215.

Gregory, T. (2001). Fear of success? Ten ways alternative schools pull their punches. *Phi Delta Kappan, 82* (8), 577–581.

Gretzinger, B. Q. (1988). System-wide implementation of an assertive discipline-based behavior management plan: A program evaluation (Doctoral dissertation, The University of Southern Mississippi, 1988). *Dissertation Abstracts International, 49,* AAC8902491.

Grumet, M. R. (1988). *Bitter milk: Women and teaching.* Amherst: The University of Massachusetts Press.

Hagborg, W. J. (1991). A follow-up study of high school students with a history of grade retention. *Psychology in the Schools, 28* (4), 310–317.

Hall, E. T. (1966). *The hidden dimension.* Garden City, NY: Doubleday & Company.

Hall, E. T. (1983). *The dance of life: The other dimension of time.* Garden City, NY: Anchor Press, Doubleday.

Hansen, J. M., & Childs, J. (1998). Creating a school where people like to be. *Educational Leadership, 56* (1), 8–13.

Hanson, S. L., & Ginsberg, A. L. (1988). Gaining ground: Values and high school success. *American Educational Research Journal, 25* (3), 334–365.

Hawkins, J. D., Farrington, D. P., & Catalano, R. F. (1998). Reducing violence through the schools. In D. S. Elliot, B. A. Hambert, & K. R. Williams (Eds.), *Violence in American schools.* New York: Cambridge University Press.

Hergenhahn, B. R. (1976). *An introduction to theories of learning.* Englewood Cliffs, NJ: Prentice-Hall.

Herman, J. L. (1992). *Trauma and recovery.* New York: BasicBooks, HarperCollins Publishers.

Hollingsworth, E. J., Lufler, Jr., H. S., & Clune III, W. H. (1984). *School discipline: Order and autonomy.* New York: Praeger Publishers.

Howard, E. R. (1978). *School discipline desk book.* West Nyack, NY: Parker Publishing Company.

Hummel, M. O. (1986). The interaction between teachers and students who are assigned to central detention (attitude, background, goals) (Doctoral dissertation, Rutgers, The State University of New Jersey, 1986). *Dissertation Abstracts International, 47,* AAC8613873.

Hyman, I. A., & Snook, P. A. (2000). Dangerous schools and what you can do about them. *Phi Delta Kappan, 81* (7), 489–498, 500–501.

Jarvis, P. A., & Justice, E. M. (1992). Social sensitivity in adolescents and adults with learning disabilities. *Adolescence, 27* (108), 977–988.

Jones, K. M., Young, M. M., & Freman, P. C. (2000). Increasing peer praise of socially rejected delinquent youth: Effects on cooperation and acceptance. *School Psychology Quarterly, 15* (1), 30–39.

Jones, V. F., & Jones, L. S. (1995). *Comprehensive classroom management: Creating positive learning environments for all students.* Boston: Allyn and Bacon.

Jozefowicz, D. M. H., Colarossi, L., Abreton, A. J., Eccles, J. S., & Barber, B. L. (2000). Junior high school predictions, high school dropout, movement into alternative educational settings, and high school graduation: Implications for dropout prevention. *School Social Work Journal, 25* (1), 31–43.

Kampol, B. (1994). *Critical pedagogy: An introduction.* Westport, CT: Bergin & Garvey.

Kaeser, S. C. (1979). Suspensions in school discipline. *Education and Urban Society, 11* (4), 465–484.

Kaestle, C. F. (1978). Social change, discipline, and the common school in early nineteenth century America. *Journal of Interdisciplinary History, 9* (1), 1–17.

Kent, R. B. (1999). *Beyond Room 109.* Portsmouth, NH: Boynton Cook Publishers.

Klaczynski, P. A. (1990). Cultural-developmental tasks and adolescent development: Theoretical and methodological considerations. *Adolescence, 25* (100), 811–823.

Kleifgen, J. (1988). Learning from student teachers' cross-cultural communicative failures. *Anthropology and Education Quarterly, 19* (3), 218–234.

Kochman, T. (1983). *Black and white styles in conflict.* Chicago: The University of Chicago Press.

Kohn, A. (1993a). Choices for children: Why and how to let students decide. *Phi Delta Kappan, 75* (1), 8–21.

Kohn, A. (1993b). *Punished by rewards: The trouble with gold stars, incentive plans, A's, praise, and other bribes.* Boston: Houghton-Mifflin.

Kordahl, E. C. (1989). Cutting patterns among learning disabled students attending a comprehensive urban high school (Doctoral dissertation, University of San Francisco, 1989). *Dissertation Abstracts International, 51,* AAC9019255.

Kratzert, W. R., & Kratzert, M. Y. (1991). Characteristics of continuation high school students. *Adolescence, 26* (101), 13–17.

Kreisberg, S. (1990). *Transforming power: Domination, empowerment, and education.* Albany: State University of New York Press.

Kreuter, K. J. (1983). Student and teacher attitudes toward disciplinary practices in a junior high setting (Doctoral dissertation, Temple University, 1983). *Dissertation Abstracts International, 44* (8), 611–618, AAC8418604.88.

Landau, B. M. (2000). *Teaching the skills of social behavior: An examination of teaching mainstream expectations to students in the margins.* Paper presented at the Annual Conference of the American Educational Research Association (New Orleans, LA, April 24–28, 2000).

Landsheer, J. A., & Win, H. H. (2000). Punishments adolescents find justified: An examination of attitudes toward delinquency. *Adolescence, 35* (140), 682–693.

Langdon, C. A. (1999). The fifth Phi Delta Kappa poll of teacher's attitudes towards the public schools. *Phi Delta Kappa, 80* (8), 611–618.

Larson, K. A., & Gerber, M. M. (1987). Effects of social metacognitive training for enhancing overt behavior in learning disabled and low achieving delinquents. *Exceptional Children, 54* (3), 201–211.

Larson, K. A., & Karpas, M. R. (1967). *Effective secondary school discipline.* Englewood Cliffs, NJ: Prentice-Hall.

Lazerson, D. B., Foster, H. L., Brown, S. I., & Hummel, J. W. (1988). The effectiveness of cross-age tutoring with truant junior high school students with learning disabilities. *Journal of Learning Disabilities, 21* (4), 253–255.

Leone, P. E., Mayer, M. J., Mamgren, K., & Meisel, S. M. (2000). School violence and disruption: Rhetoric, reality, and reasonable balance. *Focus on Exceptional Children, 33* (1), 1–20.

Lewis, R. (2001). Classroom discipline and student responsibility: The students' view. *Teaching and Teacher Education, 17* (3), 307–320.

Lickona, T. (1997). The teacher's role in character education. *Journal of Education, 179* (2), 63–80.

Lightfoot, S. L. (1983). *The good high school: Portraits of character and culture.* New York: Basic Books.

Loeber, R., & Stouthamer-Loeber, M. (1998). Juvenile agression at home and at school. In D. S. Elliot, B. A. Hambert, & K. R. Williams (Eds.), *Violence in American schools.* New York: Cambridge University Press.

Long, N. J., & Morse, W. C. (1996). *Conflict in the classroom: The education of at-risk and troubled students.* Austin: Pro-ed.

Lovegrove, M. (1983, August). *Comparative and international studies and the theory and practice of education.* Proceedings of the Annual Conference of the Australian Comparative and International Education Society. Hamilton, New Zealand.

Lovitt, T. (2000). *Preventing school failure.* Austin: Pro-ed.

Lufler, H. S. Jr. (1978). Discipline: A new look at an old problem. *Phi Delta Kappan, 59* (6), 424–426.

Lufler, H. S. Jr. (1979). Debating with untested assumptions: The need to understand school discipline. *Education and Urban Society, 11* (4), 450–464.

Mansfield, W., & Farris, E. (1992). *Office for Civil Rights survey redesign: A feasibility survey* (NCES 92-130). Westat, Inc. Rockville, MD: National Center for Education Statistics.

Martinson, J. (1991, October). *High school principals and students: Negotiating deviant behavior through politeness.* Paper presented at the annual meeting of the Speech Communication Association, Atlanta, GA.

Mates, D., & Allison, K. R. (1992). Sources of stress and coping responses of high school students. *Adolescence, 27* (106), 461–474.

McAdams, J. A. (1980). A study of compliance, attitudes, and factors influencing school principals in relation to state regulations on suspensions of students (Doctoral dissertation, Temple University, 1980). *Dissertation Abstracts International, 41,* AAC8014549.

McConaughy, S. H. (1986). Social competence and behavioral problems of learning disabled boys aged 12–16. *Journal of Learning Disabilities, 19* (2), 101–106.

McEwan, B. (1995). *Effective management practices for severely emotionally disturbed youth.* A paper presented at the Annual Meeting of the American Educational Research Association (San Francisco, CA, April 18–22).

McEwan, B. (1996). *It is as much the how as the what: Examining my own practices for teaching classroom management.* Paper presented at the Annual Meeting of the American Educational Research Association (New York, NY, April 8–12).

McEwan, B., & Gathercoal, P. (2000). Creating peaceful classrooms: Judicious discipline and class meetings. *Phi Delta Kappan, 81* (6), 450–454.

McIntosh, R., Vaughn, S., & Zaragoza, N. (1991). A review of social interventions for students with learning disabilities. *Journal of Learning Disabilities, 24* (8), 451–458.

McKay, M. M., & Stone, S. (2000). Influences on urban parent involvement: Evidence from the National Education Longitudinal Study. *School Social Work Journal, 25* (1), 16–30.

McPortland, J. M., Jordan, W., Legters, N., & Balfanz, R. (1997). Finding safety in small numbers. *Educational Leadership, 55* (2), 14–17.

Meier, D. (1995). *The power of their ideas: Lessons for America from a small school in Harlem.* Boston: Beacon Press.

Mills, M. C. (1987). An intervention program for adolescents with behavior problems. *Adolescence, 22* (85), 91–96.

Millman, H. L., Schaefer, C. E., & Cohen, J. J. (1980). *Therapies for school behavior problems.* San Francisco: Jossey-Bass.

Mitchell, M. M. V. (1989). Discipline management systems and the use of timeout (Doctoral dissertation, University of Texas at Austin, 1989). *Dissertation Abstracts International, 50,* AAC8920782.

Moore, W. L., & Cooper, H. (1984). Correlations between teacher and student background and teacher perceptions of discipline problems and disciplinary techniques. *Psychology of the Schools, 21* (3), 386–392.

Mounts, N. S. (2001). Young adolescents' perceptions of parental management of peer relationships. *Journal of Early Adolescence, 21* (1), 91–122.

Muir, M. (2000/2001). What gets in the way for underachievers? *Mainely Middle,* 13–25.

Natriello, G. (1984). Problems in the evaluation of students and student disengagement from secondary school. *Journal of Research and Development in Education, 17* (4), 14–24.

Newman, B. M., & Newman, P. R. (1987). The impact of high school on social development. *Adolescence, 22* (87), 525–534.

Nieto, S. (1996). *Affirming diversity: The sociopolitical context of multicultural education.* New York: Longman Publishers USA.

Noddings, N. (1984). *Caring: A feminine approach to ethics and moral education.* Berkeley: University of California Press.

Noddings, N. (2001). The care tradition: Beyond "Add women and stir." *Theory into Practice, 40* (1), 29–34.

Norris, T. R. (1981). Disciplinary control practices in Texas secondary schools (Doctoral dissertation, Baylor University, 1981). *Dissertation Abstracts International, 42,* AAC8120228.

Nunn, G. D., & Parish, T. S. (1992). The psychological characteristics of at-risk high school students. *Adolescence, 27* (106), 435–440.

Ogbu, J. U. (1987). Variability in minority school performance: A problem in search of an explanation. *Anthropology and Education Quarterly, 18* (4), 312–344.

O'Leary, K. D., & O'Leary, S. G. (1972). *Classroom management: The successful use of behavior modification.* Elmsford, NY: Pergamon Press.

Osborne, A. G., Jr. (1998). The principal and discipline with special education students. *NASSP Bulletin, 82* (599), 1–8.

Pares, S. G., & Pares, A. H. (2001). Classroom applications of research on self-regulated learning. *Educational Psychologist, 36* (2), 89–101.

Pasupathi, M., Staudinger, U. M., & Baltes, P. B. (2001). Seeds of wisdom: Adolescents' knowledge and judgment about difficult life problems. *Developmental Psychology, 37* (3), 351–361.

Pate, P. E., Homestead, E. R., & McGinnis, K. L. (1997). *Making integrated curriculum work: Teachers, students, and the quest for coherent curriculum.* New York: Teachers College Press.

Patterson, C. H. (1977). *Foundations for a theory of instruction and educational psychology.* New York: Harper & Row.

Patthey-Chavez, G. G. (1993). High school as an arena for cultural conflict and acculturation for Latino Angelinos. *Anthropology and Education Quarterly, 24* (1), 33–60.

Pemberton, R. R. (1985). A study of the effectiveness of in-school suspension as perceived by high school principals (Doctoral dissertation, University of Missouri, 1985). *Dissertation Abstracts International, 47,* AAC8607953.

Perry, C. L., & Duke, D. L. (1978). Lessons to be learned about discipline from alternative high schools. *Journal of Research and Development in Education, 11* (4), 78–91.

Pervil, S. (1998). Reflections. *Primary Voices K–6, 7* (2), 31–37.

Pestello, F. G. (1989). Misbehavior in high school classrooms. *Youth and Society, 20* (3), 290–308.

Phelps, L. (2000). Appraisal and prediction of school violence. *Psychology in the Schools, 38* (2).

Pinnell, G. S. (1985). The "Catch-22" of school discipline policy making. *Theory into Practice, 24* (4), 286–292.

Poplin, M., & Weeres, J. (Eds.). (1992). *Voices from the inside: A report on schooling from inside the classroom.* Claremont, CA: The Institute for Education in Transformation at The Claremont Graduate School.

Pringle, R. W. (1931). *The psychology of high school discipline.* San Francisco: D. C. Heath and Company.

Ramos, I. S. (1980). An analysis of student absenteeism based upon the perceptions of selected Rhode Island high school students within schools of high rates of absenteeism and schools of low rates of absenteeism (Doctoral dissertation, The University of Connecticut, 1980). *Dissertation Abstracts International, 41,* AAC8103229.

Ray, P. P. (1991). A study of various geographic, social and school policy factors and their relative impact on Tennessee high school attendance rates (Doctoral dissertation, Memphis State University, 1991). *Dissertation Abstracts International, 52,* AAC9214871.

Raywid, M. A. (2001). What to do with students who are not succeeding. *Phi Delta Kappa, 82* (8), 582–584.

Reed, D. B., & Himmler, A. H. (1985). The work of the secondary assistant principalship: A field study. *Education and Urban Society, 18* (1), 59–84.

Reilly, D.H. (2000). The learner centered high school: Prescription for adolescents' success. *Education, 121* (2), 219–228.

Rose, L. C., & Gallup, A. M. (1998). The 30th annual Phi Delta Kappa/Gallup Poll of the public's attitude toward the public schools. *Phi Delta Kappa, 80* (1), 41–56.

Rose, L. C., & Gallup, A. M. (2000). The 32nd annual Phi Delta Kappa/Gallup Poll of the public's attitudes toward the public schools. *Phi Delta Kappa, 82* (1), 41–66.

Rouner, L. S. (1993). Can virtue be taught in a school? Ivan Illich and Mohandas Ghandi on deschooling society. In B. Darling-Smith (Ed.), *Can virtue be taught?* Notre Dame: Notre Dame Press.

Rumberger, R. W. (1987). High school dropouts: A review of issues and evidence. *Review of Educational Research, 57* (2), 101–121.

Rupp, G. (1993). Teaching virtue turns vicious: "Political correctness" and its critics. In B. Darling-Smith (Ed.), *Can virtue be taught?* Notre Dame: Notre Dame Press.

Rusk, R. R., & Scotland, J. (1979). *Doctrines of the great educators.* New York: St. Martins Press. Sabatino, D. A., Sabatino, A. C., & Mann, L. (1983). *Discipline and behavioral management: A handbook of tactics, strategies and programs.* Rockville, MD: Aspen Systems Corporation.

Salend, S. J., & Salend, S. M. (1986). Competencies for mainstreaming secondary level learning disabled students. *Journal of Learning Disabilities, 19* (2), 91–94.

Samples, F., & Aber, L. (1998). Evaluations of school-based violence prevention programs. In D. S. Elliot, B. A. Hambert, & K. R. Williams (Eds.), *Violence in American schools.* New York: Cambridge University Press.

Schab, F. (1991). Schooling without learning: Thirty years of cheating in high school. *Adolescence, 26* (104), 839–847.

Scherer, M. (1999). Is school the place for spirituality: A conversation with Rabbi Harold Kushner. *Educational Leadership, 56* (4), 18–22.

Schoenlein, J. (2001). Making a huge high school feel smaller. *Educational Leadership, 58* (6), 28–31.

Short, P. M., Short, R. J., & Blanton, C. (1994). *Rethinking student discipline.* Thousand Oaks, CA: Corwin Press.

Skiba, R. J., & Deno, S. L. (1991). Terminology and behavior reduction: The case against "punishment." *Exceptional Children, 57* (4), 298–313.

Soltis, S. F. (1991). The application and enforcement of the compulsory attendance and truancy laws in twelve outstate Minnesota school districts and their corresponding court systems (Doctoral dissertation, University of Minnesota, 1991). *Dissertation Abstracts International, 52,* AAC9127758.

Spring, J. (1994). *Wheels in the head.* New York: McGraw-Hill.

Stanley, R. T. (1984). A study of relationships between selected student background factors of secondary school students who serve detention and the number of detentions they serve (Doctoral dissertation, Pepperdine University, 1984). *Dissertation Abstracts International, 45,* AAC8418604.

Stedman, J. M., Castillo, R. M., Gaines, T., Villareal, A., Abbott, D., & Durass, C. (1989). Achievement in an alternative high school for emotionally/behaviorally disturbed students. *Adoloscence, 24* (95), 623–630.

Steffey, S., & Hood, W. J. (Eds.). (1994). *If this is social studies, why isn't it boring?* York, ME: Stenhouse Publishers.

Stinchcombe, A. L. (1964). *Rebellion in a high school.* Chicago: Quadrangle Books.

Streng, F. J. (1993). Cultivating virtue in a religiously pluralistic world. In B. Darling-Smith (Ed.), *Can virtue be taught?* Notre Dame: Notre Dame Press.

Suleiman, M. F. (2000). *Teaching social studies multiculturally: Implications for teachers.* Portions presented at the National Social Science Association Conference (Las Vegas, NV, March 26–28).

Sullivan, C., De Carlo, C., De Falco, K., & Roberts, V. (1998). Helping students avoid risky behavior. *Educational Leadership, 56* (1), 80–82.

Sweeney, J. (1992). School climate: The key to excellence. *NASSP Bulletin, 76* (574), 69–73.

Sykora, F. J. (1981). In-school suspension—Alternatives within an option. *NASSP Bulletin, 65* (448), 119–122.

Tatum, B. D. (1997). *"Why are all the Black kids sitting together in the cafeteria?": And other conversations about race.* New York: Basic Books.

Thomas, G. W. (1989). An evaluation of the Saturday Study and Guidance School, an alternative to out-of school suspension (Doctoral dissertation, University of San Francisco, 1989). *Dissertation Abstracts International, 51,* AAC9021976.

Thomases, J. S. (1998). Challenging the norms: Democracy, empowering education, and negotiating the curriculum. *New Designs for Youth Development, 14* (3), 30–35.

Thompson, W. E., & Dodder, R. A. (1986). Containment theory and juvenile delinquency: A reevaluation through factor analysis. *Adolescence, 21* (82), 365–376.

Thorson, S. A. (1995). *Macbeth* in the resource room: Students with learning disabilities study Shakespeare. *Journal of Learning Disabilities, 28* (9), 575–581.

Thorson, S. A. (1996, November). The missing link: Students discuss school discipline. *Focus on Exceptional Children, 29* (3), 1–12.

Trzyna, G. D., & Miller, S. (1997). *A case study of learning in an integrated literature-history class: Personal narrative, critical reflection, and Kris's way of knowing.* Albany, NY: National Research Center on English Learning and Achievement.

Utley, C. A. (Ed.). (2001). Peer mediated instructions and interventions in the 21st century. *Remedial and Special Education, 22* (1).

Varney, S. S., & Cushner, K. (1990). Understanding cultural diversity can improve intercultural interactions. *NASSP Bulletin, 74* (528), 89–94.

Vélez-Ibáñez, C. G., & Greenburg, J. B. (1992). Formation and transformation of funds of knowledge among U.S.-Mexican households. *Anthropology and Education Quarterly, 23* (4), 313–335.

Vogt, L. A., Jordan, C., & Tharp, R. G. (1987). Explaining school failure, producing school success: Two cases. *Anthropology and Education Quarterly, 18* (4), 276–286.

Weber, T. R. (1984). Perceptions of superintendents, principals, assistant principals, deans, counselors, and teachers concerning discipline in selected Illinois high schools (Doctoral dissertation, Northern Illinois University, 1984). *Dissertation Abstracts International, 45,* AAC8503860.

Wehlage, G., Smith, G., & Lipman, P. (1992). Restructuring urban schools: The new futures experience. *American Educational Research Journal, 29* (1), 31–93.

Wehmeyer, M. S., & Schalock, R. L. (2001). Self-determination and quality of life: Implications for special education services and supports. *Focus on Exceptional Children, 33* (8).

Weiner, L. (1999). *Urban teaching: The essentials.* New York: Teachers College Press.

Weisner, T.S., Gallimore, R., & Jordan, C. (1988). Unpackaging cultural effects on classroom learning: Peer assistance and child-generated activity. *Anthropology and Education Quarterly, 19* (4), 327–353.

Williams, P. A., Alley, R. D., & Henson, K. T. (1999). *Managing secondary classrooms: Principles and strategies for effective management and instruction.* Boston: Allyn and Bacon.

Williams-Boyd, P., Skaggs, K., & Ayres, L. (2000). Marriage in the middle: The art and craft of teaching early adolescents. *Childhood Education, 76* (4), 236–239.

Wolfgang, C. H. (1995). *Solving discipline problems: Methods and models for today's teachers.* Boston: Allyn and Bacon.

Wonot, P. E. (1983). Social skills: An awareness program with learning disabled adolescents. *Journal of Learning Disabilities, 16* (1), 35–38.

Woolfolk, A. E. (1990). Prospective teachers' sense of efficacy and beliefs about control. *Journal of Educational Psychology, 82* (1), 81–91.

Wynne, E. A. (1990). Improving pupil discipline and character. In O. C. Moles (Ed.), *Student discipline strategies: Research and practice* (pp. 167–192). Albany: State University of New York Press.

Yeager, W. A. (1949). *Administration and the pupil.* New York: Harper and Brothers.

Young, J. T. (1991). A profile of high schools selected as high schools of excellence in the state of Georgia, 1984–89 (Doctoral dissertation, University of Georgia, 1991). *Dissertation Abstracts International, 52,* AAC9124374.

Zane, N. (1994). When "discipline problems" recede: Democracy and intimacy in urban charters. In M. Fine (Ed.), *Chartering urban school reform: Reflections on public high schools in the midst of change.* New York: Teachers College Press.